He was forced to remain in th
further into the busiest parts of London ~~~~ ~~~~ ~~~~ ~~~
when the coach reached Haymarket, Barwick realised he would be
late for work and broke off the pursuit, much to De Berenger's relief.

That same morning, Ralph Sandom sent word from
Northfleet to the Rose Inn at Dartford requesting a chaise and four.
He, together with McRae and Lyte, dressed in the French uniforms
and white cockades, and armed with the handbills, set off for their
triumphal drive through the City and then south of the river where,
either by design or a singular coincidence, they alighted at Marsh
Gate, where De Berenger had changed coaches some hours earlier.
They calmly removed their uniforms, donned hats and walked off.

De Berenger meanwhile had arrived at number 13 Green
Street – a house to which Cochrane had moved just days before –
only to be told by the servants that their master was not at home. He
was at that moment at King's factory in Cock Lane in the City,
superintending the manufacture of the prototype of his new lamp.

De Berenger asked if he might wait and sent a servant,
Thomas Dewman, out with a note asking Cochrane to return home.
Dewman first went to Cumberland Street where Cochrane had
breakfasted with his uncle but finding that his master had already
left, he came back to Green Street. He suggested that, if De
Berenger did not mind waiting, he would go to King's factory where
he felt sure his master would be found.

De Berenger agreed but took back the note and added two or
three more lines to it. Cochrane was found by his servant, the note
was delivered and he came back to Green Street. He talked with De
Berenger and lent him a hat and coat before he left.

The motive for this apparently simple act was to be gravely
disputed later and was to form the cornerstone of evidence for
Cochrane's complicity in the fraud.

Shortly afterwards, Cochrane returned to Chatham to
supervise the final preparations for the sailing of the *Tonnant*. On
the Saturday following the fraud, 26 February, Cochrane Johnstone
visited De Bergenger at his lodgings in Asylum Buildings and
handed him a letter. The following day, De Berenger cleared out his
lodgings and disappeared.

The Stock Exchange Committee was meanwhile on the trail of the fraudsters. On 4 March it posted the notice on the floor of the House asking for information on unusually heavy dealings on the day of the fraud. On 9 March its report naming Lord Cochrane, Cochrane Johnstone and Butt was published.

The affair was by now a public scandal, magnified by the press, and public opinion was violently aroused, especially when handbills were posted in the streets offering a reward for Colonel Du Bourg and telling of his being traced to Green Street.

The same day that the Committee's report was published, Cochrane quit the *Tonnant*, returned to London and, on 11 March, made a voluntary affidavit accounting for his movements on the day of the fraud and explaining his connection with De Berenger, whom he named as the only officer to visit Green Street on the day of the fraud.

In his 11 March affidavit, Cochrane gave the following account of his visitor on that day.

"Having obtained leave of absence to come to town , in consequence of scandalous paragraphs in the public papers, and in consequence of having learnt that hand-bills had been affixed in the streets, in which (I have since seen) it is asserted that a person came to my house, at No 13 Green Street, on the 21st day of February, in open day, and in the dress in which he had committed a fraud; I feel it due to myself to make the following deposition that the public may know the truth relative to the only person seen by me in military uniform, at my house, on that day.
    COCHRANE

"I, Sir Thomas Cochrane, commonly called Lord Cochrane, having been appointed by the Lords Commissioners of the Admiralty to active service (at the request, I believe, of Sir Alexander Cochrane) when I had no expectation of being called on, I obtained leave of absence to settle my private affairs previous to quitting this country, and chiefly with a view to lodge a specification to a patent relative to a discovery for increasing the intensity of light. That in pursuance of my daily practice of superintending work that was executing for me, and knowing that my uncle, Mr. Cochrane Johnstone, went to the City every morning in a coach. I do swear, on the morning of the 21st of February (which day was impressed on my mind by circumstances which afterwards occurred) I breakfasted with him at his residence in Cumberland street, about half past eight o'clock, and I was put down by him (and Mr. Butt was in the coach) on Snowhill, about ten o'clock; that I had been three quarters of an hour at Mr. King's manufactory, at No 1 Cock Lane, when I received a few lines on a small bit of paper, requesting me to come immediately to my house; the name affixed, from being written close to the bottom, I could not read. The servant told me it was from an army officer, and concluding that he might be an officer from Spain, and that some accident had befallen my brother; I hastened back, and I found Captain Berenger, who, in great seeming uneasiness, made many apologies for the freedom he had used, which nothing but the distressed state of his mind, arising from difficulties, could have induced him to do. All his prospects, he said, had failed, and his last hope had vanished, of obtaining an appointment in America. He was unpleasantly circumstanced on account of a sum which he could not pay, and if he could that others would fall upon him for full £8000. He had no hope of benefitting his creditors in his present situation, or of assisting himself. That if I would take him with me he would immediately go on board and exercise the sharp-shooters (which plan Sir Alexander Cochrane, I know, had approved of). That he had left his lodgings and prepared himself in the best way his means allowed. He had brought the sword with him which had been his father's, and to that, and to Sir Alexander, he would trust for obtaining an honourable appointment. I felt very uneasy at the distress he was in, and knowing him to be a man of great talent and science, I told him I would do everything in my power to relieve him; but as to his going immediately to the *Tonnant*, with any comfort to himself, it was quite impossible, my cabin was without furniture, I had not even a servant on board. He said he would willingly mess anywhere. I told him that the ward-room was already crowded, and besides I could not with propriety take him, he being a foreigner, without leave from the Admiralty.

He seemed greatly hurt at this, and recalled to my recollection certificates which he had formerly shewn me, from persons in official situations. Lord Yarmouth, General Jenkinson and Mr. Reeves, I think, were amongst the number. I recommended him to use his endeavour to get them, or any other friends to exert their influence, for I had none, adding that when the *Tonnant* went to Portsmouth, I should be happy to receive him; and I knew from Sir Alexander Cochrane, that he would be pleased if he accomplished that object. Captain Berenger said that not anticipating any objection on my part from the conversation he had formerly had with me, he had come away with intention to go on board and make himself useful in his military capacity; he could not go to Lord Yarmouth, or to any other of his friends, in this dress, (alluding to that which he had on) or return to his lodgings where it would excite suspicion (as he was at that time in the Rules of the King's bench) but that if I refused to let him join the ship now, he would do so at Portsmouth. Under present circumstances, however, he must use a great liberty, and request the favour of me to lend him a hat to wear instead of his military cap. I gave him one which was in a back room with some things that had not been packed up, and having tried it on, his uniform appeared under his greatcoat; I therefore offered him a black coat that was laying on a chair, and which I did not intend to take with me. He put up his uniform in a towel, and shortly afterwards went away in great apparent uneasiness of mind; and having asked my leave, he took the coach I came in, and which I had forgotten to discharge in the haste I was in. I do further depose that the above conversation is the substance of all that passed with Berenger, which, from the circumstances attending it, was strongly impressed on my mind, that no other person in uniform was seen by me, at my home, on Monday the 21st of February, though possibly other officers may have called (as many have done since my appointment) of this, however, I cannot speak of my own knowledge, having been almost constantly from home, arranging my private affairs. I have understood that many persons have called under the above circumstances and have written notes in the parlour and other have waited there in the expectation of seeing me, and then gone away, but I most positively swear that I never saw any person at my house resembling the description, and in the dress stated in the printed advertisement of the members of the Stock Exchange. I further aver that I had no concern, directly or indirectly, in the late imposition, and that the above is all that I know relative to any person who came to my house in uniform on the 21st day of February, before alluded to. Captain Berenger wore a grey great coat, a green uniform and a military cap. From the manner in which my character has attempted to be defamed, it is indispensably necessary to state that my connection in any way with the funds, arose from an impression that in the present favourable aspect of affairs, it was only necessary to hold stock in order to become a gainer without prejudice to any body; that I did so openly, considering it in no degree improper, far less dishonour-able; that I had no secret information of any kind, and that had my expectation of the success of affairs been disappointed, I should have been the only sufferer. Further, I do most solemnly swear that the whole of the Omnium on account, which I possessed on the 21st day of February 1814 amounted to £139,000 which I bought by Mr. Fearn (I think) on the 12th ultimo at a premium of 28¼, that I did not hold on that day any other sum on account in any other stock directly or indirectly, and that I had given orders when it was bought to dispose of it on a rise of one per cent, and it was actually sold on an average of 29½ premium, though on the day of the fraud it might have been disposed of at 33½ . I further swear that the above is the only stock I sold of any kind on the 21st day of February, except £2000 in money which I had occasion for, the profit of which was about £10. Further, I do solemnly depose that I had no connexion or dealing with anyone, save the above mentioned, and that I did not at any time , directly or indirectly, by myself or by any other, take or procure any office or apartment for any broker or other person for the transaction of stock affairs."

"COCHRANE"

Cochrane had this affidavit widely publicised and employed John Wright to print it and distribute it to the papers as a press release, remarking to him, "I have no reason to think that Captain De Berenger is capable of so base a transaction, but if he is I have given

the gentlemen of the Stock Exchange the best clue to find him out."
The affidavit was published in the Morning Chronicle of 12 March.

If, however, Cochrane imagined that its publication would mark the end of the affair, he was grievously mistaken: his troubles were only just beginning.

CHAPTER FOUR
Day of Settlement

"To clear a stable of rats: sending for the rat-catcher is about the worst of all plans because he will look forward to a continuation of your favours."

Charles Randon De Berenger "Helps and Hints, How to Protect Life, Property, &tc."

After the close of business of 21 February, when it became clear that a fraud had been practised on a vast scale, an air of outrage hung over Throgmorton Street. This was not the first time in recent months that attempts had been made to exploit the sensitivity of the stock market to rumour, and even by using the same device of false news of the war.

Just seven months earlier, in August 1813, a very similar trick had been attempted when a forged letter, purporting to come from an agent of the respected broking firm of Goodwin, Curling & Friend at Deal was sent to the Committee at Lloyd's. It read:-

> "Messrs. Bennett & Co., Lloyd's.
> Sirs,
> We have just time to acquaint you that one of our cruisers has this moment landed a French officer whom they picked up in a flag of truce. He is the bearer of despatches for the Government and brings passports for a British Minister. He has been taken to the port admiral to the port admiral.
> We are Sirs,
> Your Obedient Servants, Goodwin, Curling Friend & Co.
> Deal, August 6th 1813.

The receipt of this letter caused a minor rise in Government stock and a wave of buying and selling. The Committee of the Stock

Exchange had on this occasion decided to take action to find out who was responsible and formed a subcommittee for the purpose under the chairmanship of Charles Laurence, who was chairman of the Committee itself. Also on the subcommittee were Francis Baily, Benjamin Oakley and Charles Nairne, all of whom were later to play leading roles in unmasking the conspiracy of 1814.

The subcommittee posted the forged letter in the House on 14 August 1813 asking the help of Members and it sat several times in the next few weeks to sift through a trickle of information and follow up the few slender leads it gained. Suspicion fell on a Charles Johnson because the hand in which the letter was written was said to resemble his, and because he had dealt in Consols on the day in question. It eventually turned out, though, that Johnson was innocent.

On 24 August, the subcommittee posted a reward notice at Lloyd's offering £100 to anyone discovering the author of the forgery. But it got no takers for the £100 and was ultimately forced to let the incident die a natural death for lack of information. Because the affair had provoked an outcry in the City though, the subcommittee was not disbanded and nominally continued its investigations. Events were to prove the decision not only expedient but fortunate too.

in 1814, the Stock Exchange was effectively controlled by two independent committees: the Committee for General Purposes, constituted by the deed of settlement, which had the sole management of the affairs of the exchange and regulated the activities of its Members, and the quaintly but aptly named Committee for the Protection of Property against Fraud and Artifice – a private association of some of the Members. Because the General Purposes Committee had no funds of its own, it got to together with the Committee for the Protection of Property to set up the subcommittee to deal with the forged letter, voting Charles Laurence, chairman of the General Purposes Committee into the chair of the subcommittee.

Now, in February 1814, Members were to be grateful that they already had a body set up to investigate fraud, and that it had not been wound up after its disappointing investigation of the previous year.

Charles Laurence wasted no time in calling a meeting of the subcommittee for the first morning following the fraud, 22 February. At first, information was sparse and tended to be garbled and second-hand. All that they got for their first day's efforts was the statement of David Jones who had been in Rochester the day before and who was told by the landlady of the inn that "two Russian officers had changed horses at her pub, saying that Buonaparte was dead."

The next day they got much more, and they got their first suspects. Mr. Collett, a partner in the firm of Thomsett, Collett, Moule & Kelsea, told them that he went to Dover on the 19th "to get information" and Wright at the Ship Inn had told him that Bonaparte was dead. He admitted buying 26,000 Consols personally and a further 80,000 in concert with two others. Collett also gave them the name of Thomas Vinn who evidently had been dining out on his story of being approached to impersonate "Du Bourg", for the subcommittee got the same story from John Hodge who heard it from an acquaintance, and Reginald Graham who got it from Vinn himself. Finally, a Mr. Gardiner came before them and mentioned the names of Sandom, Holloway and "L. Brown".

The same day, the subcommittee posted a notice on the floor of the House appealing for information. The following day, Thursday 24, they called in a police officer, Sayer, from Bow Street, briefed him on the evidence they had so far and sent him out looking for Sandom, Holloway and L. Brown.

The subcommittee now fell victim to a misfortune to which all such bodies are vulnerable when they appeal to the public for information. They found sitting before them a plausible, knowledgeable, eager-to-please man called Peake who was so happy to be in the limelight for a change, and so anxious to stay there, that he kept the subcommittee supplied with a constant stream of "evidence". Whenever his memory became exhausted and his usefulness as a witness seemed at an end, his imagination provided the details which ensured yet another appearance before the subcommittee.

Peake told them that he had gone to Dover on the 22 February after staying at Rochester on Monday night. At Dover, he heard about the hoax in London and he found out from a messenger called Rutter who were the people responsible. Rutter, he said, had received instructions from Collett (of Thomsett, Collett, Moule & Kelsea) to forward any news "whether founded or unfounded". Consequently, whe n Rutter heard of Du Bourg from the landlord at the Ship Inn, he went straight to Thomsett with the news and sent an express messenger up to Collett.

Peake said that he himself had spoken to Thomsett and asked him, "is it true?" Thomsett's reply was that it could not be a deception because "the man had got the greyhound badge". (The official sign of a King's Messenger) On top of all this, said Peake, Thomsett held 100,000 in Omnium. He was, he told the subcommittee, firmly convinced that Collett, Thomsett, Moule and someone called Hayward were responsible. "And that," he asserted confidently, "is what everyone at Dover Believes."

After this diversion, the subcommittee came back to earth with an interview with Thomas Vinn who related his encounter with Alexander McRae. At this stage, the subcommittee clearly believed that they had their "Du Bourg" in McRae. It was the helpful Mr. Peake who had given the first description of the Dover impostor as being about 40, with peaked chin, roman nose and 5 foot 9 inches tall. Vinn now nodded his agreement to the subcommittee's yes, McRae is about 40; yes, he has a peaked chin; yes, a roman nose.

McRae was, said Vinn, a clerk to a person in St. Martin's Lane, Cannon Street – a wine seller named Holloway. This was the second time in two days that the name Holloway had come up and the subcommittee now decided that the Sandom/Holloway tip-off was a hot lead which should be run down. Sayer, the policeman, went after Sandom and discovered that he was a prisoner within the Rules of the King's Bench but was nowhere to be found.

Charles Laurence went in person with Vinn to Holloway's in Cannon Street where the clerk told them his master was not in. They went on to the Carolina coffee house where the waiter confirmed that Holloway and McRae came in every day. It was not only Vinn who, from being initially a suspect, became converted to the role of amateur detective. Anxious to clear himself of Peake's accusations, Collett tracked down the post boy, Foxall Baldry, who drove the "French officers" and Baldry told him that he had recognised one of his passengers – it was Ralph Sandom.

On Saturday 26 February, the subcommittee got its first really big break. They found William Crane, the hackney cab driver, and Thomas Shilling, who drove "Du Bourg" up from Dartford to London. Crane gave a detailed account of picking up Du Bourg at the Marsh Gate and of his dress: a brown greatcoat trimmed with fur, a red coat under it and a sword which was on the seat of the coach. The man himself "looked like a foreigner", had a florid complexion and a cough. Shilling told of his long drive up from Dartford with a passenger who had a large red nose, a blotchy face, and whose eyes seemed to have a nervous twitch.

Shilling added that his fare chose to lend a little dramatic authenticity to his role by leaning out of the window and saying, "this is a delightful morning. Ah! Old England! I have not seen you a long time before." The man wore a brown surtout, a red coat under it and had a sword and a very small portmanteau on the seat.

Joseph Fearn, the stockbroker, was summoned before the subcommittee. He told them indignantly he did not imagine any of the people he did business for had any hand in the fraud. He denied knowing Holloway, McRae or Sandom, and said he neither knew nor did business for Thomsett. He did know Lord Cochrane and Mr. Cochrane Johnstone and had done business for them. Mr. Cochrane Johnstone, he said, took the office for him in Shorter's Court. Altogether, he sold some 900,000 of Omnium and Consols.

Fearn's clerk, Thomas Christmas, was brought before the subcommittee and questioned about changing banknotes at Bond's bank. (The Stock Exchange had been given the notes spent by Du Bourg at Dover, by the Home Office, where they had been sent by the Surveyor of Customs). The nervous young clerk appeared to prevaricate. He could not say that he did not change them, and he would not swear that he did.

Fearn was hauled back again. His clerk was evidently concealing something and this time Fearn was questioned in detail about his dealings for Lord Cochrane, Cochrane Johnstone and Butt;

about the amounts bought and when; how much they sold and whether they had acted in concert or independently.

A Clerk from Bond's bank was sent for and asked in the presence of Christmas whether he could identify the person who changed four £10 notes and two £5 notes at his bank on Saturday 19 February. He pointed out Christmas, who broke down under questioning and admitted that he was sent to Butt's office in Sweeting's Alley by Fearn on the Saturday to report the latest stock market prices: Butt asked him to change the notes at the bank, and he agreed: he took the changed notes back to Butt and gave them to him.

Now Fearn was brought back yet again, but this time he was armed with the first piece of ammunition for the counter attack against the subcommittee. It was a letter from Cochrane Johnstone.

> "18 Great Cumberland St. 1st March 1814
> Dear Sir,
> I understand that a committee of the Stock Exchange has demanded of you what quantity of stock you sold for me last week. Although I believe that you, as a broker, take an oath of secrecy not to disclose the names of your employers and that such questions put to you by the committee was highly improper to give it no other term, still however with the threat which I am informed was held over you that the committee would expel you from their body if you did not answer, I do as far as I am concerned approve of your having answered any questions applicable to myself and you are at perfect liberty to give to the committee any statement which they may require of my concerns with you.
> I am authorised also on the part of Lord Cochrane to do the same.
> I am Sir,
> Your Obedient Servant,
> A. Cochrane Johnstone.
> Mr. Fearn, Stockbroker.
> You are at liberty to read this to the committee."

In the meantime, the irrepressible Peake was back filling the subcommittee's ears with yet more incredible revelations and Thomas Vinn reported some progress in tracking down McRae. He was, Vinn said, hiding up at or near Gosport.

The subcommittee now made another attempt to reach Sandom, this time through his attorney, Highmore, but the lawyer knew little about Sandom except that a Mr. Holloway had been his bail in an assault case. (Holloway's name once more, noted the subcommittee.)

Charles Laurence asked him to try to get Sandom to come before the subcommittee and testify, on the promise of a reward. As for Highmore himself, his incentive to persuade Sandom to talk would be the prospect of being employed in any legal steps they took.

By now, a week had elapsed since the fraud had been carried out and the subcommittee had made solid progress: they had the broker who had sold most of the stock on the day of the fraud and the names of his principals. They had the names of the sub-plotters although they had not yet got a line on them.

Also "Colonel Du Bourg" still eluded theme This defect was remedied on Friday March 4 when Michael A. Gorman was introduced to the subcommittee by Charles Nairne. Gorman announced dramatically, "I know the man!"

"He is about 5 feet 10 high with foxy hair, has a squint and a nervous catching in his eyes. His eyes turn inwards. He is about 40 and is a man capable of doing such business."

Gorman said he had sent the man out in a ship of his and the fellow had behaved infamously, pretending to be a French officer and sporting a croix. He was, said Gorman, an ex-army man whose real name was James Bourke but who called himself "Du Bourg".

On the same day, the subcommittee posted a notice on the floor of the House requesting an interview with any Members who had transacted business on 21 February for Andrew Cochrane Johnstone, R.G. Butt, Lord Cochrane, or messrs Holloway, Sandom or McRae.

Meanwhile Sayer, the Bow Street runner, had been busy doing a little undercover work in Green Street. He went to the public house there, bought himself a drink and engaged the landlord in friendly conversation. The house in Green Street, it seemed, belonged to a Mr. Durand and had been let furnished to Lord Cochrane who lived there "with his brother and three or four men."

Sayer probed a little deeper and was told that the servant who had opened the door to Du Bourg had been "turned off". He had been sent into the country and another servant hired in his place.

Moreover, confided the publican, the serving maid was being kept out of the way. Sayer tried out the description of Du Bourg's uniform on the landlord. Had he ever seen anyone at Number 13 wearing clothes of that description? The innkeeper was unsure but his attention was arrested by the fur cap with gold trimmings. Mr. Durand, he said, sometimes wore a similar cap.

On Saturday 5 March, the subcommittee approved and ordered to be printed a notice offering a reward for the discovery of Du Bourg, whom they recognised as the key to the whole affair.

250 GUINEAS REWARD DEATH OF BUONAPARTE
Whereas the person who represented himself as Colonel R. Du Bourg and as having arrived at Dover from the coast of France at about one o'clock in the morning of 21st February with a false report respecting the death of Buonaparte, proceeded in a post chaise and four from the Ship Inn, Dover, towards London and stopped at the Marsh Gate, Lambeth, where he took a hackney coach and was set down and entered the house
No. 13 Green Street, Grosvenor Square
about half past nine o'clock on the same morning, this is to give notice that whoever will give the first information to the committee of the Stock Exchange so that the above mentioned person may be identified shall receive 50 guineas reward, and upon conviction of the offender a further reward of 200 guineas.
The above person is described as being of the middle size having large whiskers, rather prominent nose, complexion somewhat red, dressed in regimentals with a fur cap trimmed with a gold lace band and a brown surtout coat

trimmed with fur and worked with a silk cord of the same colour. When at Dover prior to his appearance at the Ship Inn he threw away a black silk round hat which was picked up the next morning and may be seen at the committee room of the Stock Exchange.

March 5th 1814.

Shortly after approving the draft advertisement on Saturday the subcommittee at last got its first glimpse of a conspirator in the flesh. Holloway had been persuaded to talk. He was courteous, helpful and frank. If he knew anything about the fraud, he explained, he would be happy to disclose it. But the fact is, he knows nothing. No, he does not know Lord Cochrane or Mr. Cochrane Johnstone. Yes, he does know Alexander McRae who is a debtor of his and a man in distressed circumstances.

No, McRae is not an employee but merely someone he occasionally sends on errands and gives money to out of a sense of charity. Ralph Sandom, he said, had told him that two men came to him at Northfleet in a boat on the morning of 21 February and that was all he knew.

The subcommittee's investigations now took a rather extraordinary turn. The indefatigable, if plodding Sayer returned to them after expending yet more boot leather running down several leads and in particular exploiting his productive contact with the landlord and customers of the pub in Green Street. As Sayer read over his notes to them, it was clear that a startling theory was beginning to take shape.

Lord Cochrane, said the policeman, had moved into Green Street on Thursday 17 February. At 3.30 on that Thursday morning, Lord Cochrane or someone else from No. 13 travelled in a chaise down to Dartford. This story was enlarged on by Thomas Shilling, the Dartford post boy, who told the subcommittee that one of his fellow drivers picked up a fare at Green Street the previous night (Friday 4 - Saturday 5) at one o'clock in the morning and drove him to Dartford, from where the person went on to Rochester. Shilling and the other driver had compared notes and the man driven to Dartford corresponded with the description of Du Bourg. When he left Green Street, he told another man at the door to wait there until he received a letter.

Clearly, the theory was beginning to emerge that Lord Cochrane himself was Du Bourg, or that someone hiding out at Cochrane's house in Green Street was Du Bourg – either the Mr. Durand who had let the house, or one of the "three or four men" who, according to Sayer, were living there. Equally clearly, the worst side-effects of offering to pay for evidence not taken under oath were beginning to cloud the subcommittee's investigation as the eager and inexperienced post boy, Shilling, found both popularity and reward in passing on the kind of information he believed the subcommittee wanted to hear.

This latest round of evidence convinced Charles Laurence that the Stock Exchange had enough information to act on, and together with Nairne, Lewis and Baily, he went to Whitehall with a copy of the minutes to see Lord Sidmouth, the Home Secretary.

While Sidmouth may well have been impressed with the Stock Exchange's findings, he was not sufficiently persuaded to agree that the Crown should undertake the prosecution. While the rest of the subcommittee was out, Joseph Fearn asked on behalf of Cochrane Johnstone for one of the reward advertisements, but Messrs Hammond and Wakefield, who had been left in charge of the office, told him that they did not have one to spare.

After the weekend, on Monday 7 March, Sayer came up with another link in the chain of evidence he was forging to support the "Green Street hideout" theory.

One of his contacts had told him that the steward of Cochrane's ship, the *Tonnant*, was a foreigner whose description tallied with that of Du Bourg's. Now Laurence and a deputation of the subcommittee met Lord Melville, First Lord of the Admiralty, by appointment at 4 o'clock.

While he received noises of sympathy from the Admiralty, though, he again got no tangible offer of support beyond the offer of advice on the legal aspects of the case from the Attorney General. Meanwhile, Ralph Sandom, sensing a profit in the air, had been making overtures towards the subcommittee. Through an intermediary he told them that he would be willing to come forward, provided that the price was right.

Through his attorney, Highmore, he said that he did not know either Cochrane or Cochrane Johnstone and that he had never bought or sold on the stock market. Eventually, Sandom agreed to parley, and on the next day, tuesday 8 March, Holloway brought him before the subcommittee. His story was truly extraordinary. At between 5 and 6 o'clock on the morning of 21 February, he said, two men came to his house in Northfleet in a galley rowed by six sailors, saying they had come from France. They brought with them a pencilled note from a Mr. Partridge apparently on a leaf torn out of a packet book, which read,

"Mr. Sandom,

These gentlemen have come recommended to me. I request you will go with them to London. Don't ask them for any money." Thinking that Partridge was on board the galley, Sandom called out, "Partridge, come out and have some grog." But the men said, "no, we're going to Gravesend and shall get something there." The two men who landed wore the dress of French officers white cockades in their hats. They hardly said twenty words to him and in any case spoke only French although when they got to London later, he discovered that they did in fact speak English.

When Sandom asked them what the news from France was, they wrote down, "Les. Alliez a Paris, Le Tyrant Blessie, Vivent les Bourbons." Sandom sent to Dartford for a chaise and they drove to London together. As they passed through the City, he suggested they stop at the Mansion House to deliver the news, but the men said they wanted to go straight to the Prime Minister, Lord Liverpool.

They took a boat at Westminster Bridge to go to Whitehall Stairs. When they disembarked, the men led him down a passage, up a flight of stairs and dismissed him with the words, "we do not want you to come any further."

In reply to questions, Sandom declared that he did not know nor had he ever seen, Lord Cochrane, Cochrane Johnstone or Richard Butt. Asked if he had not told a Mr. Hall that "if the committee would give him £1,000, he would tell all", Sandom reacted with injured innocence. He had never said any such thing, he declared. Showing a nice turn of Euphemism, he told the subcommittee that being temporarily financially embarrassed had deprived him of his liberty for three months. But he had now paid all his debts – not, he hastened to add, since 21 February.

Why then, the committee wanted to know, did he think that he had been singled out to be made unwittingly a party to the fraud?

"Being a man of frolicsome disposition," replied Sandom, "I suppose someone thought me a proper person to practise a trick upon."

Later that day, 8 March, the subcommittee was due to present its findings to its parent committees, and now busied itself marshalling the evidence so far garnered. But first it had one more witness to hear: a routine informant who had come forward like so many others in response to newspaper reports.

William Harrison was introduced to the subcommittee by John Granville. Harrison said he had read in the papers a description of Du Bourg and that he knows a man who was in the Prussian army and who corresponds with the description. He has large whiskers, said Harrison, a prominent nose, and something particular in his eyes. He is about 40, a stout made man and a foreigner who is in the Rules of the King's Bench but who breaks his rule. He is intimate with Lord Cochrane and Cochrane Johnstone and is hardly a day without dining with the latter – who, Harrison added confidentially, is not worth a shilling.

The man lives at Alsop's Buildings on the New Road. His name is Berenger. He is a Prussian, is very ingenious and is putting up some baths for Cochrane Johnstone. The routine report went into the files, along with Michael Gorman's and was forgotten.

At a joint meeting of the General Purposes Committee and the Committee for the Protection of Property later that day, Charles Laurence read the subcommittee's report and told the assembled committee members of his visit to Lord Melville at the Admiralty.

Melville had told him, he said, that "if they had any occasion for legal advice, they might apply to the Attorney General. " David Ricardo, the eminent economist and a member of the committee, congratulated Laurence and suggested that the report might be printed, but without mentioning the amount of which investors had been defrauded. Ricardo knew the Stock Exchange was a long way down in public esteem following the recent frauds, and he was worried that revealing the full extent of the losses would bring them down even further and quite possibly depress stock levels. His motion was carried unanimously.

At 4 o'clock that afternoon, the doors of the Stock Exchange were locked, all strangers excluded and a table was pulled to the centre of the floor of the House. Hushed Members gathered round the table as Charles Laurence climbed onto it and read the report. David Ricardo then made a speech described in the Morning Chronicle next day as "very animated" in which he said that the Stock Exchange "generally laboured under all the opprobrium of any foul transaction when, in fact, they were the chief persons injured by such nefarious practices." The investigation, he said, could not be made too public as it might operate to deter any other desperate characters from trying similar attempts. He therefore moved that the whole of the report be printed.

Here was an undisguised hint to those Members who had lines of communication into the daily papers to get maximum publicity for the successful detection of the conspirators, and some Members took the hint. In the papers next day, paragraphs appeared, most of them wrong in matters of detail and some wildly inaccurate. In attempting to protect the image of the Stock Exchange, Ricardo was condemning the suspects to trial by the media.

In its report which squarely pointed the finger at Cochrane, Cochrane Johnstone and Butt, the Exchange noted, "although the subcommittee in thus presenting the results of their labours may be considered as virtually dissolved, yet they beg leave to state that they are ready and willing to continue their exertions as long as they may be considered necessary.

They are in possession of still further information on the subject which it is considered proper not to disclose at present and which they hope and expect will eventually crown their efforts with complete success." This show of confidence, though, was partly bluff and was aimed at getting the suspects rattled.

The only other information the subcommittee had was the deposition of Alexander McRae's neighbour who told them of the

Scotsman's buying two French officer's uniforms, and they still had some way to go before they could rightly consider themselves as "virtually dissolved".

On Friday 11 March, the irrepressible Peake appeared once more before them just long enough to mention that he had a new suspect. It was, he said, the harlequin of Drury Lane Theatre.

Peake's real reason for coming was to ask for the return of written allegations he had left with the subcommittee some days earlier, a request with which the secretary advised them to comply. The secretary went to the lengths of tearing the page containing the allegations out of the minutes – evidently Peake's imagination had run riot and come up with accusations too scurrilous to remain on record.

With his papers clutched in his hand and his tail between his legs, Peake decided that he had enough of fighting the cause of justice and disappeared back into obscurity. No doubt the subcommittee felt relieved to be rid of him.

March 11 was the day Cochrane made out his affidavit naming De Berenger, and gave it to John Wright to be printed and distributed to the press. Evidently the subcommittee got hold of a copy of the affidavit the same day.

That some Members wrote paragraphs for the papers – or had press contacts – is shown by the publication of the subcommittee's confidential report the morning after it had been read behind locked doors, so the Stock Exchange may have got a copy of Cochrane's affidavit through its contacts with the press. Possibly Wright, or even Cochrane himself sent them a copy. At any rate, it is clear that they saw it on Friday 11 because they promptly ordered their newly appointed solicitor, Germain Lavie, to apply for a writ of *habeus corpus* for De Berenger.

The date and the connection are important. It shows that it was Lord Cochrane's affidavit that put them onto De Berenger as Colonel Du Bourg.

Lavie's clerk, Chatfield, was sent away to apply for the writ but returned a little later and said that on consideration he thought that "some obstacle might lie in the way of obtaining it." What the "obstacle" could have been is not clear, but the subcommittee nevertheless pursued their enquiries for De Berenger who they were now convinced, was Du Bourg.

Next day, Saturday, David Ricardo brought up a thorny problem which had been giving the subcommittee some sleepless nights – the £8,000 or so profit made by people suspected of being parties to the fraud. For an organisation whose motto was My Word Is My Bond not to honour the bargains made on 21 February was unthinkable; it could even precipitate a flight from stock investment from which the Exchange would never recover. In Ricardo's words, "the Stock Exchange will pay all it has lost: but it will not consent that it should go into the pockets of the persons with whom the fraud might have originated."

As a way out of this dilemma, Ricardo proposed that the money be deposited in trust until such time as the suspects proved their innocence. If they were unable to do so within six months, the money would be given to charity. This resolution was put to the House and passed unanimously.

By Monday 14 March, just three weeks after the fraud, the subcommittee now had virtually all the information it needed and was largely concerned with tying up the loose ends. De Berenger's lodgings in Asylum Buildings were visited, but he was gone and the scent was cold.

A Picadilly gunsmith called Hewson told the subcommittee that on 25 February De Berenger visited his shop and surprised him by paying off an account outstanding for three or four years. He wanted to buy, said Hewson, a rifle which he intended to present to Lord Cochrane, "to whom he was under obligations".

But if the subcommittee was for the moment marking time, the matter was far from closed, and now appeared in the *Morning Chronicle* the opening shots in a fierce battle of words which was to rage throughout March and April. On 14 March the *Chronicle* carried a letter from Cochrane Johnstone

"No. 18 Great Cumberland Street March 12th 1814
Mr. Editor,
    Although the public newspapers have been filled of late with statements affecting my character originating from

the members of the Stock Exchange committee, I have thought it to be my duty to remain silent until the report daily promised from that committee shall be printed and that I should be put in possession of it. Having this day seen it by accident, for it is only circulated among their own body, although it was the bounden duty of the committee, if they had been men of honour, to have sent me a copy of it, I can no longer refrain from publicly contradicting the infamous and unfounded statements contained in the said report, which can be done upon oath by the very parties stated by the committee to have given them the information. I have instructed my solicitors immediately to adopt those measures which my counsel may deem proper in order that justice may be done to my character and to punish those who have dared to put their names to the most unfounded statements which malice could invent, and which they must have known to be false at the moment they were affixing their names to the report.

A. Cochrane Johnstone."

In defence of their honour, at least, Cochrane Johnstone and Richard Butt appeared to be acting in concert since the same paper carried a remarkably similar letter from the stock jobber. He, too, said he had delayed replying to the "infamous and gross falsehoods" in the papers until he had seen a copy of the report and went on to positively deny the accuracy of the report.

His solicitors, said Butt, had "received orders from me instantly to commence a prosecution against the committee of the Stock Exchange for inserting falsehoods as infamous and unfounded as ever appeared in publication".

The *Chronicle* that day carried another letter from Cochrane Johnstone, an open letter to the committee of the Stock Exchange, declaring the amount of profit made by him, Cochrane and Butt. These, he pledged himself to prove, were: Lord Cochrane £1,700, Butt £1,300 and himself £3,500. In the same letter he threatened to be preparing for the press a correct statement of all the stock bought and sold on the day of the fraud with the names of the people dealing.

Lord Cochrane, too, joined battle in replying to a rather scurrilous paragraph that had appeared in the *News* of 13 March purporting to show that De Berenger's much-quoted appointment to the *Tonnant* was a blind, since the ship already had a capable officer in its major of marines, Major Nicholls. The simple answer was that De Berenger's appointment was applied for and rejected before Major Nicholls had been appointed to fill the position. In the *Chronicle* the next day, Cochrane replied to the report of the subcommittee and its allegations of a cover-up.

> "13 Green Street, Grosvenor Square, 14th March 1814
> To the Editor of the Morning Chronicle.
>
> Having learnt from several of my friends that it would be satisfactory if, in addition to my deposition which was sent forth before I had seen the report of the committee of the Stock Exchange, I were to explain the circumstances relative to my servants, which is involved in obscurity by the evidence of Sayer, the police officer. I beg leave to state that, so far from an intention to conceal anything that might be passing in my house on the 21 February, the fact is that I had actually two sets of servants there, one set who had just come, and another who were about to leave me having had a month's previous warning. As to the man sent to the country, he was to relieve my sea steward and is now in charge of my house at Holly Hill. The other manservant is in town and both can be called on.
>
> I have also to add that no other man as stated by Sayer, except my servants, lived in my house, and that the maidservants are forthcoming, although they did not think proper to converse with suspicious looking people who have at times endeavoured to intrude themselves. It seems to me that there is now no point unanswered except the purchase of the Napoleons, which upon application to Mr. Binn will prove to be totally unfounded.
> Cochrane."

The reference to gold Napoleons was inspired by a paragraph in the *Chronicle* of 7 March asserting that Cochrane had bought French gold from a dealer in Threadneedle Street immediately before the fraud.

In the Chronicle of 22 March was a parliamentary report of Cochrane's Johnstone's defence of himself in the House as Member for Grampound.

"Mr. Cochrane Johnstone rose from a sense of what was due to his own character, and more especially as a Member of the House, to contradict those statements which had appeared in the public prints implicating him in the imposition that had lately been practised in the money market. For the present he should content himself with solemnly declaring that those statements were utterly unfounded and that he had no hand in, and no knowledge of the fraudulent transaction in question. That it was his intention to publish in a few days a statement which would be found fully to confirm the declaration he now solemnly made to the House."

The statement he promised in the House was also referred to in a trailer for the forthcoming issue of Cobbett's Political Register for 26 March, in which, said Cochrane Johnstone, would be published a clear statement of everything with respect to himself."

On 23 March, the Chronicle carried a long article written by Cochrane and supported by affidavits which he had collected from his servants, Thomas Dewman, Isaac Davis, and Mary Turpin, and from William King who was the manufacturer of his patent lamp and Samuel Thomas of Binns & Co., who deposed to never having sold Cochrane any gold Napoleons.

The substance of the servants' affidavits was that the collar of De Berenger's uniform when he called at Green Street was green, not red as stated by Crane and Shilling in the Stock Exchange report. Cochrane also attacked Sayer's statement that servants had been "turned off" or kept out of the way to supress evidence, and that three or four men lived at his house in Green Street.

All the servants swore that no-one lived there except Cochrane and his servants, and their affidavits confirmed that the coming and going of servants was a legitimate part of the normal run of domestic life. The *Chronicle* story also had some caustic remarks to make about police methods and pointed to Mary Turpin's second affidavit which said;

"I, Mary Turpin, now maidservant with Lord Cochrane do swear that on Friday 18th March Inst. between the hours of one and two o'clock of the forenoon of the said day a boy servant to Mr. Collingwood, greengrocer in Green Street, Grosvenor Square, came to me and informed me that a lady wanted to speak to me at his master's house. That I went there immediately and found a lady just within the street door of Mr. Collingwood's, that the said lady told me a gentleman wanted to speak to me, that I went to the gentleman, he took me a few yards on to the corner of North Audley Street, that the person asked me what sort of uniform the person wore who came to Lord Cochrane's house about three weeks ago, that I thinking it wrong to give him any information at all, told him that I could not tell him. "Oh yes you can," said he, "if you choose, and if you will, I will give you £5." That the gentleman repeated this offer five or six times, that I did not take any money from him. Then he went away with the lady, that the lady stood by within hearing of the conversation but said nothing."

On the day that these affidavits appeared, the investigation was brought to life again as far as the subcommittee was concerned when Du Bourg1s scarlet uniform and insignia were fished up from the river by a Thames waterman, George Odell, while dredging for coal. The coal he found on this occasion had been used, together with some pieces of lead and metal screws, to send the incriminating garment to the bottom of the river. On the 24 March, a notice was posted in the Stock Exchange advertising the find and a week later, on 30 March, two subcommittee members paid a visit to Solomon's shop in Charing Cross where the uniform was identified. Solomon said that the purchaser, "Mr. Wilson", brought with him a brown leather portmanteau "about 20 inches or two feet long and 10 or 12 inches broad" in which the articles were packed.

Once having resurrected itself, the enquiry now moved again into top gear. In early April the subcommittee got its first line on De Berenger when it was handed a letter written from Sunderland by an un-named quaker to his friend in London.

"Sunderland April 1st 1814

Dear Joshua,

A gentleman calling himself Major Burn, having as he says a commission in the Swedish Army, has been staying at the Bridge Inn here about a fortnight, and from several circumstances has been suspected to be the famous, or rather infamous, Captain Berenger. Indeed, I have just learnt that a gentleman named Hewstler, formerly a wine merchant in London and now resident here, declares that he knew Berenger in town, had arrested him for debt once and that this person is the man.

This Major Burn appears to me to be about 45 years of age and about 5 feet 7 or 8 inches high, pale face a little pitted with smallpox, is an excellent draughtsman. He has with him a beautiful bugle-horn such as are used by officers of rifle corps and trunks are marked "CB". He has applied here for a passage to Holland in a collier. He was too late in his application, the vessel had sailed, but he was informed by the shipbroker that another would be ready in about 10 days. He went to Newcastle yesterday in a post chaise, telling the landlord he meant to return in a few days after visiting Tynemouth. I have set one of our police officers, an intelligent fellow but not equal to Bow Street, on the scent. He will follow him to Newcastle in the morning and apply to a magistrate there for a warrant to take him into custody.

Now, do the gentlemen of the Stock Exchange wish him taken? Or does Lord Cochrane and Co. wish it? I am of opinion that thou wilt think with me that there are strong circumstantial evidence that this is the man. I have never seen any reward offered for the apprehension of Berenger or any description of his person which will account for the questions I have asked, and thou wilt please therefore write to me by first post, and say what had best be done in the case, and as soon as I hear anything from the officer I shall inform thee. My only fear is that he, Berenger, has got a ship at Newcastle and is off."

Later, in their brief to counsel, the subcommittee noted that "on this letter being handed to the committee they waited upon Lord Sidmouth, Secretary of State for the Home Department and his Lordship immediately decided to issue his warrant for the apprehension of De Berenger under the authority vested in him by the Alien Act."

It will be seen later that this claim cannot be reconciled with the evidence given at the trial. The warrant for De Berenger's arrest was actually issued by the Home Secretary on 17 March, five days after Cochrane's affidavit naming his visitor appeared in the papers. Now that the subcommittee had a lead on De Berenger's whereabouts, Joseph Wood of the Alien's Office set out on April 4 armed with the warrant to track down the fugitive. He travelled to Sunderland, traced him northwards to Newcastle and Glasgow, and eventually got his man at Leith on the Scottish coast on April 8, attempting to take ship for Holland under his alias of "Major Burne".

Back in town, the suspects were carrying on their war of words against the subcommittee in the papers. Butt wrote to the *Chronicle* enclosing letters which he had sent to the Stock Exchange demanding to know what had happened to their profits from 21 February, letters which had been ignored. Now he ran to earth one of the trustees of the profits and started legal proceedings against him for the return of the money. On 11 April, however, De Berenger was brought back to London and was initially kept in custody at the house of Joseph Wood, the Alien Office agent, for interrogation.

The subcommittee was taking no chances of him being got-at in the free and easy atmosphere of a public jail. The conspirators panicked at De Berenger's arrest and the plot now began to break wide open. On 12 April, Andrew Cochrane Johnstone wrote a truly extraordinary letter to Charles Laurence:

"No. 18 Great Cumberland Street 12th April 1814
To the Chairman of the Committee, Stock Exchange
Sir,
I have this moment received a letter, of which the enclosed is a copy, and lose no time in transmitting it to you for the information of the gentlemen composing the Stock

Exchange Committee; from the bearer of the letter, I am given to understand that Mr. McRae is willing to disclose the names of the Principals concerned in the late hoax, on being paid the sum of £10,000 to be deposited in some banker's hands, in the names of two persons to be nominated by himself, and to be paid to him on the conviction of the offenders.

I am happy to say, that there now seems a reasonable prospect of discovering the authors of the later hoax, and I cannot evince my anxious wish to promote such discovery more than by assuring you that I am ready to contribute liberally towards the above sum of £10,000 and I rest assured that you will eagerly avail yourselves of this opportunity to effect the proposed discovery (an object you profess to have so much at heart) by concurring with me in such contribution.

I have the honour to be, Sir, Your obedient humble servant, A. Cochrane Johnstone."

The enclosed letter from McRae read:

"April 12th
Sir,
I authorize the bearer of this note to state to you that I am prepared to lay before the public the names of the persons who planned and carried into effect the late hoax practised at the Stock Exchange the 21st February, provided you accede to the terms which my friend will lay before you.
I am, Sir,
Your obedient servant, A. McRae.
To the Honourable Cochrane Johnstone."

To the messenger who delivered these remarkable letters, Charles Laurence said, "give my services to Mr. Johnstone and I will report the business to the committee on Saturday next, when they meet." The letters were in fact laid before the Committee for

General Purposes who found the subject "too absurd for them to listen to, or even send any answer."

Getting no reply, Cochrane Johnstone now dashed off a stream of letters to the Morning Chronicle alleging that the Stock Exchange had turned down McRae's offer because "the disclosure will affect persons of great respectability and fortune much connected with the Stock Exchange and who profited above £50,000 by the hoax suggested by them." He even went to the lengths of having the letters printed as placards which he stuck up in the City streets and in the avenue leading to the Exchange.

On 18 April, Cochrane Johnstone wrote again to Charles Laurence.

> "18 Great Cumberland Street
> 18th April 1814
>   Sir,
>   I have to request that you will be so good as to inform me what are the intentions of the Stock "Exchange on the subject of the letter which I addressed to you relative to the proposal of Mr. McRae. Lord Cochrane, Mr. Butt and myself are willing to subscribe £1,000 each in aid of the £10,000 required by Mr. McRae. The bearer waits your answer which, to prevent any mistake I hope you will find time to commit to writing.
>   I am,
>   Your obedient servant,
>   A. Cochrane Johnstone.

> To Mr. Charles Laurence
>   Chairman of the Committee of the Stock Exchange."

To James Stokes, the clerk who delivered the letter, Charles Laurence replied, "give my services to Mr. Johnstone and tell him it is not from any unpolite motive I do not write an answer but I am desired not to commit pen to paper on any account whatever. I will lay his letter before the Committee when they Meet and they will communicate to Messrs. Hitchens and Fearn, his stockbrokers, who will let Mr. Johnstone know the result."

The result, which Fearn passed on to Cochrane Johnstone, was that "the committee has no answer to return.".

By now, in any case, it was too late for such manoeuvring to be of any help, since the conspirators were fast deserting the sinking ship. On 25 April, Holloway with Henry Lyte in tow, went before the subcommittee and confessed. Evidently they had got wind of what Cochrane Johnstone and McRae were up to and confessed partly in the rather naive expectation of receiving a reward for saving the Stock Exchange £10,000, and partly in an attempt to secure immunity from prosecution. They were to be disappointed on both counts, possibly because they refused or were unable to implicate Cochrane Johnstone, Richard Butt or Lord Cochrane.

In the presence of Nairne, Baily, Chaumette and Wakefield of the subcommittee, with Germain Lavie sitting in, Holloway admitted to being the principal in the "Northfleet plot". He said that Ralph Sandom, Henry Lyte and Alexander McRae were the men who rode in the chaise through the City.

He only undertook it, said Holloway, because he was being persecuted for debts and he hoped to make a little money by the rise in the stock market. He never expected the results to be so serious or he would never have got involved. Lyte confirmed his testimony.

Now at last the Stock Exchange had enough hard evidence to take legal action against the conspirators. Despite repeated applications to Lord Sidmouth and to the Admiralty, however, the Home Office refused to get involved and eventually the Stock Exchange itself had to bring a prosecution against the suspected parties to the fraud, footing a bill estimated at £3,000 to do so.

On 27 April, they preferred an indictment against the conspirators and the Grand Jury for the City of London, sitting at the Old Bailey, returned a true bill against Charles Random De Berenger, Lord Cochrane, Andrew Cochrane Johnstone, Richard Butt, Ralph Sandom, Alexander McRae, John Holloway and Henry Lyte on a charge of conspiracy to defraud.

CHAPTER FIVE
Court of King's Bench

"Strategems should be called into aid when taken at a disadvantage."

Charles Random De Berenger Helps and Hints, How to Protect Life, Property &tc."

June 8 1814 was a blazing hot day. Guildhall was crowded and stifling, its courtroom packed to overflowing, as the public flocked to witness the most spectacular trial of the day: The King Against Charles Random De Berenger And Others. It was the "others" they had come to see.

Because the indictment had been removed to the Court of King's Bench, the defendants were not required to be present in person and Cochrane chose to show his contempt for the proceedings by spending the day attending to his lamp patent. His lawyers no doubt felt that the presence of the fire-eating sailor could do nothing to increase his chances of acquittal and might well prejudice the jury against him.

The principal defendant, De Berenger, was however in custody and was present in court since the case would turn on his identification. The public was not to be denied its spectacle despite the defendants not appearing in person, for gathered in court were the brightest and most distinguished legal talents of the period.

The prosecution was led by John Gurney, later Baron Gurney, member of a well-known quaker family and holder of a large and successful criminal practice. Supporting him were William Bolland a practised financial and City lawyer and equally well-known at the criminal bar, and John Adolphus, celebrated both as a historian and as an Old Bailey advocate. The main defence team – for Lord Cochrane, Cochrane Johnstone and Butt – was led by William Best, afterwards Lord Wynford, and recently. appointed

Attorney-General to the Prince of Wales. Best was supported by the distinguished team of Topping, Scarlett and Henry Brougham, later to become Lord Chancellor. De Berenger was defended by Park and Richardson; the sub-plotters Sandom, Holloway and Lyte by Messrs. Williams and Denman, while Alexander McRae was in the hands of Peter Alley.

It was, perhaps, to be expected that there would be a certain element of friction between the two sides quite apart from the normal rivalry between prosecution and defence since, some time before, Alley and Adolphus had fought a duel. The argument between the two men had been "commenced in the court with briefs wielded as bludgeons, continued in the robing room with umbrellas, and finally settled with pistols on the sands of Calais."

Before the trial began and after much debate it had been decided on a joint defence, De Berenger's answer to the charge being an alibi for the day of the fraud. Cochrane met with his counsel seven times during May and early June and at first a separate defence was advised. The problem was, of course, that a separate defence was tantamount to a partial admission of guilt and Cochrane could not be persuaded to ditch his uncle and Butt. He may even have still entertained some doubts as to De Berenger's guilt.

At any rate, his attitude to the trial was his customary mixture of arrogance and naivety, and once more his intransigence in the face of opposition won out over a more reasoning and politic course of action, and he decided to tough it out, confident that he, at least, would be acquitted. Two days before the trial, he met with all the counsel on the case who unanimously recommended a joint defence.

The case was tried before the Lord Chief Justice, Lord Ellenborough. Edward Law was son of the Bishop of Carlisle, who went the rounds of the Northern circuit and took silk in 1788. It was in that year that he made his name as an advocate when – still relatively unknown – he defended Warren Hastings at his impeachment. Long after the Parliamentary rhetoric of Hastings' accusers – Fox, Burke, Sheridan and Grey – had run out of steam, Law was still patiently and meticulously reciting the minutiae of dry, factual evidence. His concern for detail and his skilful handling of the case ultimately won out over the tide of hysterical fervour on which impeachment proceedings had originally been launched, and he secured both an acquittal for Hastings and a high reputation for himself in legal circles.

His popularity was considerably less thereafter in Parliamentary circles where the Whigs were slow to forget their defeat at his hands over the Hastings affair. In 1801 he served at Attorney General under Addington's administration and the following year became Lord Chief Justice. In 1806 he made an error of judgement when he agreed to serve for a year in Fox's cabinet of All The Talents on the death of Pitt at a critical stage of the war. For the rest of his life he was accused of being a legal tool in the hands of the Tory establishment.

It may perhaps be more accurate to say that he was a man who in peaceful times would have been a strict dispenser of justice, but who in times of widespread civil unrest and prolonged war became a stern reactionary who set his face against what he considered to be the subversive influences of radical politics and republicanism. At any rate, he earned a reputation as a tough judge and one who, if he though an accused person guilty, said so.

The jury in the case was a special panel and consisted of City of London merchants. Many of the twelve were well-known names in the world of commerce and were selected partly for their ability to grasp the details of a complex financial fraud.

At the same time it is reasonable to suppose that a group of dyed-in-the-wool City businessmen would take a strong view of such a crime, especially since some of them, or their companies, may well have been investors in Government securities themselves.

The indictment contained eight counts and boiled down to the effect that the defendants were charged with unlawfully conspiring to cause a temporary rise in the public funds by spreading false intelligence of Bonaparte's death and an allied victory in France.

The trial began at 9 o'clock in the morning and when Lord Ellenborough was seated, the court had been stilled, and the indictment read, Gurney rose to open the case for the prosecution.

His lengthy address was brilliant both for its eloquence and for its presentation and made a strong impression on the jury. The impression may have been strengthened still further by the fact that Gurney was permitted by Lord Ellenborough to address the jury from within the bar – a privilege reserved to King's Counsel. Perhaps the Lord Chief Justice was anticipating events: for Gurney would shortly get his K.C. for the successful prosecution of the case.

He first drew attention to the nature of the evidence in a trial for conspiracy. "Gentlemen, where I undertake to prove them to be guilty, you will not expect that I shall give you proof by *direct evidence*, because in the nature of things, direct evidence is absolutely impossible – they who conspire do not invite into the chamber in which they form their plan any persons but those who participate in it; and therefore, except where they are betrayed by accomplices, in no such case can positive and direct evidence be given.

But you may prove their guilt as conclusively – perhaps more satisfactorily – by circumstantial evidence. If direct and positive evidence were requisite to convict persons of crimes, what security should we have for our lives against the murderer by poison? No man sees him mix the deadly draught, avowing.his purpose. No, he mixes it in secret, and administers it to his unconscious victim as the draught of health; but yet he may be reached by circumstances."

With this chilling picture of the sinister poisoner, mixing his deadly draught, firmly fixed in their minds, the jury were then introduced to the defendants.

"Gentlemen, the first person whom I shall have to present to you as bearing a principal part in this conspiracy, the main agent of its execution, will be proved to be the defendant, Charles Random De Berenger; he was a fit person to be selected for this purpose – he was a foreigner by birth; he had resided long in this country; he would pass very well for an officer; he had been fourteen or fifteen months a prisoner in the King's Bench, or rather within the rules of the King's Bench; he would be a convenient man afterwards to convey away as he would prefer a residence in any other country because his creditors resided in this."

Gurney then outlined De Berenger's appearance at Dover, his false uniform and his imposture as Colonel Du Bourg with dispatches from France. He described the effect of the news on the Stock Exchange and the wild scramble to buy Omnium and Consols.

He next turned to the subplot of the "French officers" and the activities of Alexander McRae in approaching Thomas Vinn to impersonate an officer and getting from him the wording for his handbills, and of Sandom and Lyte in riding through the City in mock triumph.

The jury now grew attentive as Gurney marshalled his papers and turned to the meat of the case. "Gentlemen, the enquiry (of the Stock Exchange committee) respecting the chaise from Dover led to much more important results. It was the first business of the committee to learn to what place this pretended Du Bourg went in the hackney coach from the Marsh-Gate. They found out the hackney coachman, and he informed them that he was directed by Du Bourg, and he did drive straight and direct to No. 13 Green street, the house of Lord Cochrane and, it is not an immaterial consideration in this matter, a house in which Lord Cochrane had resided but three days, and a person must have been on intimate terms with Lord Cochrane to know where he resided on Monday, Lord Cochrane having gone into the house only on the Thurday evening preceding."

Gurney next told the jury of the Stock Exchange's enquiries into the stock dealings of Cochrane.

"They pursued their enquiries upon that subject and they discovered, to their utter astonishment, that this nobleman – this officer highly distinguished in the navy, then lately appointed to an important command, and one should have supposed his whole soul ingrossed in preparation for the active and important service on which he was going the Representative in Parliament for the City of Westminster, bound by the most sacred of all duties not to involve himself in any situation by which his honest judgement could be warped, and his Parliamentary conduct influenced – they found Lord Cochrane to have been a deep speculator in Omnium; that he had been so for one week only; that on the Monday morning he had a large balance on hand, and that on the Monday morning he sold out the whole of the balance, and sold it at a profit."

"When the Committee had learned thus much, they could not but feel that it was impossible that it could be an accidental co-incidence that this impostor, Du Bourg, should have alighted at the house of a person thus deeply interested in the success of the imposition which he had practised. But their enquiries and discoveries did not end there; they found that Lord Cochrane had not acted alone in these stock proceedings; that he was connected with two other persons who were still more deep in them, the one his uncle, Mr. Cochrane Johnstone (also a Member of Parliament) and the other a Mr. Richard Gathorne Butt, formerly a clerk in the Navy Office. They discovered that these persons were engaged together in speculations of a magnitude perfectly astonishing."

The prosecutor now summed up the connection between the three men with wry humour. "You have these persons, then, linked together in such a manner as will render them perfectly inseparable in these various stock transactions; having dealt for some little time; having bought and having sold; having this tremendous balance[3] this world of stock, under which they were on the Saturday evening bending and groaning, on the Monday morning they disburthened themselves completely with a profit of little more than ten thousand pounds. If the telegraph had worked, that ten thousand would have been nearer a hundred thousand – that the telegraph did not work was not to be ascribed either to them or to their agent."

This then was the burden of the prosecution case: That De Berenger would be identified as Du Bourg, that De Berenger had gone straight to Cochrane's house still wearing his false scarlet uniform and insignia, a house to which Cochrane had just moved; that Cochrane and his uncle were on intimate terms with De Berenger and that together with Butt they had speculated heavily, contracting for large amounts of stock just before the fraud and unloading their stock on the morning of the fraud. Why had De Berenger driven to Cochrane1s house?

Simple, replied Gurney. "They who contrive schemes of fraud cannot always provide for all possible events." There is always some tiny detail overlooked in their plan. In this case, the conspirators had forgotten to provide De Berenger with a hideout when he arrived back in Town. He dared not go to his lodgings still dressed in his false uniform so he went to Lord Cochrane's to get a change of dress – a change which he actually did get.

But Gurney had still more items of damning evidence. Cochrane Johnstone had hired a new suite of offices conveniently near to the Stock Exchange immediately before the fraud and a letter would be produced in his own hand in which he complained of there being other tenants in the building, "which is rather awkward, and makes it too public."

On top of this, Cochrane Johnstone had very foolishly attempted to deny having taken the house during the committee's investigations.[4] The other evidence connecting the defendants with the fraud was that when De Berenger was arrested at Leith he had in his possession banknotes traceable to Cochrane Johnstone, Butt and Lord Cochrane.

Gurney concluded, "Gentlemen, I have given you the best assistance in my power to understand and apply the evidence which will be laid before you. They whom I represent have no wish but that justice should be done. They have investigated this subject with great care, with great assiduity, with great diligence, with great anxiety. They have had no personal difference with any of these defendants; they have never come in collision with them, to have the smallest possible difference. They have no wish but justice, and I am sure that at your hands they will attain that justice; and your verdict today (which I am sure after you shall have heard the whole of this case will be a verdict of guilty) will be a salutory verdict.

It will shew the world that as there is no man beneath the law, so there is no man above it. It will teach evil-minded persons, the absurdity of expecting that schemes of fraud can be so formed as to provide for all events. It will teach them that no caution can insure safety; that there is no contrivance, that there is no device, no strategem which can shield them from detection, from punishment, and from infamy."

On this stirring note of indignation, Gurney closed his address and began to present his evidence. The first batch of prosecution witnesses, the post chaise drivers and innkeepers on the

Dover road, were called to identify De Berenger as Colonel Du Bourg, and to identify his uniform. Admiral Foley was called to tell the court of his reaction to the "victory" dispatch, which he refused to telegraph to London, not only because of the misty weather, but also because he could not believe its contents.

Instead he sent it to Croker at the Admiralty by post. Germain Lavie took the stand as being the only witness present sufficiently familiar with De Berenger's handwriting (he had interviewed him in custody) to give an opinion on the handwriting of. the Du Bourg dispatch, which he enthusiastically swore was the defendant's. Although accepted by the court, the evidence on this point was far from satisfactory.

Gurney next called George Odell, the waterman who had fished up the scarlet uniform and badges from the river. Simeon Solomon, the Charing Cross military outfitter, identified the uniform but could not swear to the identity of De Berenger, though pressed hard by both Gurney and Lord Ellenborough.

Mrs. Abigail Davidson, a fellow resident of De Berenger's in Asylum Buildings, testified to seeing Cochrane Johnstone call on De Berenger on 26 February, the Saturday after the fraud, to deliver a letter and to De Berenger's quitting his lodgings the following day.

The identification of De Berenger by a stream of witnesses was very convincing. At one stage, when there was a skirmish between Gurney and defence counsel Park over whether De Berenger was holding his head down to avoid recognition, Lord Ellenborough commented, "the questions might go much nearer; the witness might be asked if that be the person; it is always done at the Old Bailey in cases of life and death, where the prisoner stands in a conspicuous situation – it is less strong in that case; but to be sure when it is proved in the way it has been, it can be of very little consequence."

This was bad news for the defence. If De Berenger was not identified as Du Bourg, the whole prosecution crumbled: if, conversely, the identification was proved, all the defendants were placed in a weaker position. De Berenger's counsel were sufficiently worried at the position to send out the memorandum:

"We both agree in thinking that if we were to attempt the *alibi*, it would not only be of no avail against the body of proof now given, but would probably end in the witnesses being committed to Newgate; and when the day of punishment comes, making or attempting to make such a defence will probably enhance that punishment by the addition of the pillory. No power on earth can prevail in this case, if the prosecutors prove the rest of the case; and we dare not, in justice to our client, allow him to heap greater destruction upon himself without raising our warning voices against so mad a project.

J.A. Park, J. Richardson."

The underplotters – as Gurney called them with obvious relish – were quickly disposed of, especially since Holloway and Lyte had already spilled the beans to the Stock Exchange committee.

Vinn told of his mysterious meeting with McRae at the Carolina coffee house and of the Scotsman's proposal. Philip Foxall, Innkeeper of the Rose at Dartford, produced a letter written by Sandom ordering a chaise for the Monday and described the departure of the "French officers".

Evidence was then called of the defendants' stock dealings. The many small brokers that Butt and Joseph Fearn had used were put on the stand but since most of the transactions they carried out were "time" bargains – illegal in 1814 – they trooped through the court respectfully declining to answer questions on the grounds that they might incriminate themselves, and the court was left little the wiser, except concerning the standards of conduct and integrity prevailing in the City. However, Francis Baily of the Stock Exchange had privately gathered from all the brokers beforehand the extent of their dealings on behalf of Butt and the Cochranes, and entered in evidence tabulated accounts.

The Stock Exchange accounts showed Cochrane Johnstone to have bought and sold Omnium between February 8 and February 19 in parcels ranging from £10,000 to more than £300,000. His sales during the same period ranged between £10,000 and £210,000. By the Saturday before the fraud he had accumulated £420,000 of

Omnium, of which he sold off £410,000 on 21 February. During the same period, he bought and held £100,000 in Consols but did not dispose of them on 21 February.

Butt's account was shown as similar in pattern but on a smaller scale. On 21 February, he sold £224,000 of Omnium (£24,000 more than he actually possessed) and £168,000 in Consols.

Lord Cochrane confined himself to buying Omnium alone and was shown as buying £100,000 worth on 12 February, buying and selling smaller lots in the interim and finally selling the whole of his balance, £139,000.

Gurney now played his Ace. He called in evidence Cochrane's own affidavit of 11 March and proceeded to heap scorn on Cochrane's story and to pull it to pieces, in order to implicate him and De Berenger. In his address, Gurney had said of the affidavit, "Lord Cochrane has complained that he was not called upon by the Committee of the Stock Exchange to give his reasons personally. It appears to me that he has no reason to complain that they did not so call upon him – would that he had been so called upon; what would any man have given to be present to see whether any human countenance was equal to the grave relation of this extraordinary story?"

And again, "Lord Cochrane came forward with a declaration in a manner which, I confess, appears to me most degrading. If a person of this rank thought fit to give any declaration, I should have though that the mode of giving it would have been under the sanction of his honour.

Lord Cochrane thought otherwise, and he chose to give it under the half and half sanction of a *voluntary affidavit.* I call it so, gentlemen, for this reason, that although he who makes a voluntary affidavit attests his God to its truth, he renders himself amenable to no human tribunal for its falsehood, for no indictment for perjury can be maintained upon a voluntary affidavit."

It was Cochrane's affidavit which proved his own undoing. In it he describes De Berenger as calling at his house in a *green* uniform. The uniform of De Berenger's regiment, the Duke of Cumberland's Rifles was green, with a red collar. "Du Bourg" wore a scarlet uniform. If De Berenger is proved to be Du Bourg, he should therefore have appeared before Lord Cochrane in a uniform which was not that of his own regiment and with decorations to which he was not entitled; surely a suspicious circumstance? And yet far from informing the authorities immediately, Cochrane actually gives him a change of clothes.

In Gurney's words, "Mr. De Berenger tells him he cannot forsooth *'go to Lord Yarmouth or to any other of his friends in this dress.'* Why, I beg to know, cannot Mr. De Berenger go to Lord Yarmouth or any other nobleman or gentleman in the dress in which he waits upon Lord Cochrane?

If he was dressed as Lord Cochrane describes, there could be no impropriety; but still more, *'or return to his lodgings, where it would excite suspicion,'* coming out of his lodgings in this dress might be sure to excite suspicion, for persons who saw him might imagine that a gentleman thus dressed was going a little beyond the Rules of the King's Bench, but how could his return excite suspicion? If he was returning to his lodgings why would he want any other dress? Except that he was afraid to return to his lodgings in that dress because it would afford the means of tracing and detecting him."

"Gentlemen, I am sorry to find that my Lord Cochrane, filling the high situation that he does see nothing wrong in assisting a person within the Rules of the King's Bench to abscond, for whose stay within those walls sureties have entered into a bond; either Lord Cochrane's mind has confounded all right and wrong, or what is more probable, he confesses this smaller delinquency to conceal the greater, for I say he would not have made this acknowledgement unless he had to conceal that he lent the dress for another purpose, for which purpose I say De Berenger resorted to him, and which purpose was answered by Lord Cochrane's assistance."

Gurney's eloquence and his ridicule of Cochrane's story of the change of dress went home to the jury. The advocate now turned his attention to the banknotes found on De Berenger when he was arrested. Of these he observed, "All these banknotes Mr. De Berenger has desired to have returned to him. The prosecutors thought that one banknote for one pound was as good as another banknote for one pound, and in order that Mr. De Berenger might not complain of being cramped in pecuniary matters they gave over to him notes of corresponding value. But that does not satisfy Mr. De Berenger; he wants the very identical notes taken from him; he has contracted an affection for them, I suppose, on account of their having been his travelling companions.

They were his solace in a long journey, and the support to which he looked in future in a foreign land. What harm can these notes do to Mr. De Berenger? He is much too deeply implicated in this to make the presence or the absence of these notes of the least consequence to him. Who can be so blind as not to see, in the *pretended anxiety* of Mr. De Berenger for these notes, the *real anxiety* of his fellow conspirators; who, having made him their instrument in the fraud, wish now to make him their instrument in the destruction of the evidence."

Gurney then called William Smallbone, one of Butt's subsidiary brokers, who testified to giving Lord Cochrane a cheque for £470 19s 4d in payment on the stock account on 19 February. On the same day, a clerk at the bank on which it was drawn, paid the cheque with one note for £200, two for £100, a £50 note and smaller notes and coin. Cochrane later paid his coal merchant, Thomas Parker, with the £50 note. On 24 February, Smallbone's clerk, Benjamin Lance, took the two £100 notes to the bank at Butt's request to change them for £1 notes, which he took back and gave to Butt. Forty nine of these £1 notes were found in De Berenger's possession. On the same day, 24 February, Joseph Fearn sent his clerk to the bank, first to change the £200 note into two for £100 and subsequently into smaller bills.

Fearn testified that these notes he gave to Butt, who in turn handed them over to Cochrane Johnstone. Sixty seven of this batch turned up in De Berenger's effects. That, said Gurney, was the evidence for the prosecution.

By now it was 10 o'clock at night and the court had been sitting for 13 hours.

Defence counsel Best rose to say, "I wish to apprize your lordship that I think it will be necessary for the defendants to call witnesses."

In 1814, defendants in criminal trials frequently did not call any witnesses, not only because they would be subject to cross examination, but also because calling them gave the right of reply to the prosecution, leaving them with the last word.

Throughout the presentation of the prosecution evidence In this case, the defence had been making its final decision whether to call witnesses or not. De Berenger's counsel had written the note trying to dissuade him from attempting an alibi, while several times defence counsel had attempted to introduce evidence – for example of handwriting that should properly have been introduced by means of defence witnesses.

The possibility of the defence not calling any evidence was also one of the reasons that Gurney had entered Cochrane's own affidavit. Best's meaning now, therefore, was to the effect that it had been a long day; another day at least would be needed because the defence had decided to call witnesses; so this would be an opportune moment to have the adjournment.

Lord Ellenborough turned him down, however, saying, "I should wish to hear your opening and get into the defendants' case if I can; there are several gentlemen attending as witnesses who, I find, cannot without the greatest public inconvenience attend tomorrow."

De Berenger's counsel, Park, also tried to have the case divided at this point. "The difficulty we feel, I am sure your lordship will feel as strongly as we do the fatigue, owing to the length of our attendance here; but we will proceed if your lordship desires it."

Ellenborough remained unmoved, though: "I would wish to get into the case, so as to have the examination of several witnesses, upon whom the public business of certain offices depend, gone through if possible."

"I have undergone very great fatigue," persisted Mr. Park, "which I am able to bear; but I would submit to your Lordship the hardship upon parties who are charged with so very serious an offence as this, if their case is heard at this late hour; and then a fresh day is given to my learned friend to reply."

All that Park got for his persistence was a joke from the Lord Chief Justice; "it will not be a fresh day when you will be here by nine O'clock, and the sun will be up almost before we can adjourn; I will sit through it if you require it, rather than that."

Serjeant Best opened for the defence and addressed the jury on behalf of Cochrane, Butt and Cochrane Johnstone. He first apologised to the jury for keeping them still later and spoke of the importance of a full understanding of the question before them to his clients, whose careers might be ruined.

Best agreed with Gurney that the crime was a serious one and agreed also that it was a case which would be decided largely on circumstantial evidence. Where he disagreed with Gurney, he told the jury, was in denying that there were any circumstances that brought home the crime of conspiracy to his clients.

"Gentlemen, whether Mr. De Berenger be the Colonel Du Bourg who pretended to bring the news from France, or not, is not for me to discuss; I shall leave that question to my learned friend Mr. Park who, I hope, will be able to satisfy you that Mr. De Berenger is not that Colonel Du Bourg; If he is not that Colonel Du Bourg, then there is no evidence against either of the parties I represent. But admitting, for the purposes of presenting the case to you which I am called upon to support, that De Berenger is Du Bourg, still it is another question whether either of these defendants were connected with De Berenger; and I do, notwithstanding what has been said to you by my learned friend, that he was perfectly certain that he could bring home the guilt charged by this indictment to all the defendants, submit most confidently that there is no evidence against either of my clients."

First, Best examined the case against Lord Cochrane. It was, he said, that Cochrane had sold £139,000 of Omnium on the morning of the fraud and that De Berenger was at his house on that morning. Although it had been suggested by Gurney that some of the notes found on De Berenger would be traced into the hands of Lord Cochrane, the prosecution had not traced a single note to him.

The only evidence involving Cochrane with banknotes was that Benjamin Lance put into his hands two £100 notes which were later changed into £1 notes some of which were found on De Berenger. But although the £100 notes were for a time in Cochrane's hands, the same witness testified to having got them back from

Cochrane to take them to the bank for Mr. Butt. And it was to Butt that he gave the smaller bills.

"Gentlemen, I am sure therefore, that if I have made myself understood on this part of the case, I have completely released Lord Cochrane from the effect of this evidence, for though the two large notes were once in his hands, these notes were never in the hands of De Berenger. The notes found on him were the small notes given in exchange for them at the bank, and these were given to Mr. Butt, not to Lord Cochrane."[5]

Having "disposed" of the banknotes, Best moved on to the two remaining pieces of evidence. With regard to Cochrane's sale of Omnium, Best was of the opinion that the Committee of the Stock Exchange had conducted themselves unfairly because they had manipulated the evidence. They had instructed Gurney to say, and Gurney did say, that Cochrane began his speculations only a week before the fraud.

In fact, Cochrane had speculated in Omnium since the previous November, had sold as large sums before, and continued to buy and sell down to the period of the fraud. Moreover, Butt was under standing instructions from Cochrane to sell whenever a rise of one per cent occurred and it was on a one per cent rise that they were actually sold. Cochrane had not issued any special instructions for that day and was, in fact, not even in the City, but was at King's factory, busy with his lamps.

"Gentlemen, the only remaining point relative to Lord Cochrane is this, that on the Morning of the 21st February, Mr. De Berenger went to the house of his lordship. Gentlemen, it is material for your consideration how the Stock Exchange got the knowledge of that fact. Gentlemen, but for my Lord Cochrane, it is impossible that the Stock Exchange could have instituted this prosecution, because it was by Lord Cochrane1s affidavit only that the name of De Berenger was given to them.

I am aware that my learned friend stated to you, that the Stock Exchange had some reason to suspect that a Mr. De Berenger had been engaged in it before this affidavit was published; but, gentlemen, my learned friend has offered no proof of the grounds of such suspicion; the only proof that he has offered upon the subject, is the proof that my Lord Cochrane's affidavit furnished him with. Now, gentlemen, I have a right That to say, that the mere circumstances of Lord Cochrane's introducing the name of De Berenger for the first time, in that affidavit, is of itself sufficient to repel the inference arising from the circumstance of De Berenger's going to his house."

Best now went through the affidavit clause by clause, weighing Cochrane's statements against evidence already before the court and that to be presented by defence witnesses:

Cochrane went to King's factory; that he received a note asking him to come home and was told it had come from an officer; that imagining it to be an officer from Spain, where his brother was serving, he hurried home expecting news; that he found instead De Berenger who had previously applied to him to go to America to drill the sharpshooters and that De Berenger now renewed his application to go on board the *Tonnant.*

"We have it in evidence that Mr. De Berenger did expect to go to America, under the protection of Admiral Cochrane and Lord Cochrane; the narration in the affidavit is thus confirmed by this evidence; the affidavit then goes on to state that Mr. De Berenger had told Lord Cochrane, that he had left the King's Bench, and come to Lord Cochrane for the purpose of going to America. That he, Lord Cochrane, stated to De Berenger that it was impossible for his lordship to take him, that his wardroom was full; and further that De Berenger being a foreigner, his lordship could not take him without the consent of His Majesty's Government; that he might go on board ship at Portsmouth; but in the meantime he must get the permission of His Majesty's Government, upon which his lordship says, De Berenger said he would go to the noble lord, whom I have the honour to see in court,[6] to get that permission; his affidavit then states, that De Berenger said to his lordship, I must take a great liberty with you, for it is impossible I can go to the First Lord of the Admiralty in the dress in which I now am; upon which he, Lord Cochrane, not suspecting that Mr. De Berenger had been making an improper use of the dress he had on, or his views in wishing to change it, furnished him with a coat and hat."

Best now attacked the prosecutor for having made an observation prejudicial to Cochrane's case that was not borne out by the facts. "He says, did Lord Cochrane think it a right thing for his lordship to do, to furnish De Berenger with the means of escaping from his creditors? Gentlemen, there was no such thing thought of at the time, as the escaping from the King's Bench prison; the cloaths were to enable De Berenger to go to the Admiralty and to Lord Yarmouth; and it was for the purpose of appearing before Lord Yamouth and Lord Melville, that this change of dress was asked for, and not for the purpose of escaping out of the kingdom and avoiding his creditors; whether Lord Cochrane was wise or not in acceding to that request, it is not for us to decide today; but I am sure you will feel that it was straining the English law too much to say of a good tempered English sailor, that he is guilty of a conspiracy, because he yields to a request to which a person more hacknied in the tricks practised upon them would not have acceded."

If the prosecution could show, Best went on, that the contents of the affidavit were false in any respect, that would discredit the whole. But far from offering any evidence of falsehood, all the evidence corroborated Cochrane's story: yet the prosecution still asked the jury to disbelieve Cochrane's sworn statement.

Best next threw in a couple of reasoned arguments for Cochrane's innocence. First, why didn't De Berenger go to Cochrane Johnstone's house if there was a conspiracy? It was just round the corner. Again, how comes it that De Berenger sends a note to Cochrane asking him to return home at the very moment he is supposed to have been consummating the fraud in the City? These weak points clattered on stony ground. Now Best turned almost casually to the colour of the uniform.

"Gentlemen, it has been stated that the affidavit is false in that it states that Mr. De Berenger when he came to Lord Cochrane's had on a green coat, whereas it is proved by several witnesses that he had on a red one; but let me suppose that their account as to the colour of the coat is true and that Lord Cochrane's account is incorrect; would such a mistake, for it is impossible that it could be anything but a mistake, weaken the credit due to Lord Cochrane.

Men do not commit crimes unless compelled to the commission of such by some strong motive; what object could Lord Cochrane possibly have for stating that this gentleman came in one colour coat rather than another? Gentlemen, I think I can account for the mistake; my Lord Cochrane made this affidavit a great many days, I think some weeks, after the transaction had taken place.

Mr. De Berenger belonged to a corps of riflemen in this country commanded by Lord Yarmouth, and the proper dress of Mr. De Berenger as a member of that corps, was a green uniform; My Lord Cochrane had often seen Mr. De Berenger in this green uniform. His Lordship, when he made his affidavit recollected the circumstances of Mr. De Berenger's being dressed in a military uniform but there being nothing to fix on his Lordship's mind the colour of the uniform, the sort of dress in which he had been accustomed to see Mr. De Berenger presented itself to his Lordship's mind, as the dress De Berenger wore when his Lordship saw him last."

On the case of Cochrane Johnstone, which he next turned to, Best made rather similar observations: that he had speculated for months and not merely, as the prosecution suggested, for days; that he had held much larger balances previously and that he actually reduced his balance from £615,000 to £420,000 before the fraud.

Yes, he had gone into the City on the morning of the fraud – just as he went into the City every morning. Moreover, his profits on that day were even less than those gained four days earlier. The hiring of the offices in Shorter's Court could have nothing to do with a fraud which would be all over in less than an hour and for which no office was required. As for Cochrane Johnstone's calling on De Berenger on Saturday 26 February, all that is proved is that Cochrane Johnstone called on and was acquainted with De Berenger – a fact which was not in dispute.

The banknotes Best accounted for very simply; the jury had already heard of Cochrane Johnstone's plan to build "Vittoria" on the site of Alsop's Buildings and of De Berenger being employed to draw up the plans. The banknotes were simply part of the payment for his services.

Best was equally brief in the case of Butt. He, too, was a long term speculator and had held and sold large stock balances before. He had made £1,300 on the day of the fraud but had made much more on previous occasions. There was not one atom of evidence to connect him with De Berenger. Of course some of the notes in De Berenger's possession could be traced to Butt since he acted partly as Cochrane Johnstone's financial agent, making payments to him from the stock account and these notes were simply part of the payment Cochrane Johnstone had made for the work done on Vittoria.

"Gentlemen, with respect to Mr. Butt there is not a tittle of evidence bringing him into connection with De Berenger; no man has proved that ever they were seen in the same room; no person has ever brought them into connection together; and it is merely because Mr. Butt is a great purchaser of stock, and some of Mr. Butt's money is found passing through the hands of Mr. Cochrane Johnstone into the hands of Mr. De Berenger, that you are desired to find them all connected together in this conspiracy."

At around midnight, Park rose to address the jury on behalf of De Berenger. He apologised for his fatigue, remarking that it was now sixteen and a half hours since he had left home, and urging the jury not to allow their tiredness to distract their attention from the evidence.

Park soldiered bravely through De Berenger's case as he had been briefed, but there was little that could be done. His client was still determined to attempt the alibi, in the face of some of the most convincing proof of identification ever seen in a court of law. He was visibly in difficulty in presenting the alibi under the stern eye of Lord Ellenborough, who had already made it plain in his remarks that Du Bourg was De Berenger, and he tied himself up in knots in opening the matter to the jury.

"Now Gentlemen, upon the subject upon which I am about to address you, I do not think it absolutely necessary to go into it and I should not at this late hour of the morning call evidence, but in a matter so highly penal as this is, and where I am placed in so delicate a situation, and in which, thank God, I can very seldom be placed, I do not think it right to act upon my own judgement, where my client assures me that he was not the man, and is an innocent person; and that he is determined (because he knows perfectly well that what he says is the truth) to have his witnesses called; he shall have those witnesses called, for I chuse to have no responsibility cast upon me that does not belong to my situation. Gentlemen, I shall prove to you most completely that which will dispose of the case, if it is believed.

I trust I have already shown, that it is a case depending on such frail testimony, as it stands, that it is not worth any degree of credit. But I am instructed that I shall be able to call five or six witnesses, who all saw this gentlemen in London, at an hour which was impossible consistently with the case for the prosecution, and who have no interest, and had better means of knowledge than those who have been called before you."

"Gentlemen, I am quite aware, though I have not practised a great deal in criminal courts, that the evidence of an *alibi*, as we call it, is always evidence of a very suspicious nature: it is always to be watched therefore . . . "

While the prosecution without question had him by the short hairs, De Berenger could be forgiven for wondering whose side Mr. Park was on.

Park's only course was to try to discredit the prosecution's witnesses to the identity of Du Bourg on the grounds that they saw him in darkness, and Germain Lavie's handwriting testimony on the grounds that he had not known the defendant long enough. But the honest advocate felt compelled to add, "Shilling's evidence, I admit, is as to his seeing him in daylight, and his evidence is extremely strong undoubtedly."

Serjeant Pell, speaking on behalf of Sandom, Holloway and Lyte, took the only course open to him and pleaded that the conspiracy in which his clients were involved had nothing to do with the conspiracy charged in the indictment; that the "Northfleet plot" was an entirely different one, and his clients were thus innocent of the charges!

When Pell finished his address it was 3 o'clock in the morning. The court had been sitting for no less than eighteen hours.

Ellenborough now adjourned, saying, "I cannot expect your attendance before ten o'clock."

When the court re-convened the following day, the defence witnesses took the stand, first on behalf of Cochrane. Lord Melville, First Lord of the Admiralty, and Henry Goulburn, Undersecretary of State for the Colonial Office, were called to confirm that Admiral Sir Alexander Cochrane had repeatedly requested De Berenger for the American Station and had been turned down.

William King confirmed that Cochrane had been at his factory attending to his lamps between 10 and 11 o'clock, that he received a note from his servant and that he replied, "very well, Thomas." The man servant, Thomas Dewman, related De Berenger's arrival at Green Street at about 10 o'clock and his taking the note first to Cumberland Street and then to King's factory. He reported Cochrane's reaction to the note as "well, Thomas, I will return."

A witness from the Adjutant General's office confirmed that Cochrane's brother was with the army in the South of France and was notified as being "sick present" on 25 January. Finally, the fact of Cochrane's lamp patent was proved.

Witnesses were then called to substantiate Cochrane Johnstone's claim that he paid De Berenger £200 in February for work done on the plans for the Vittoria gardens and for having a prospectus printed, and that he lent De Berenger a further £200 against his oil patent scheme.

Gabriel Tahourdin, De Berenger's solicitor (and also Cochrane Johnstone's) produced correspondence on these payments and also testified that the Dover dispatch was not in De Berenger's handwriting – a statement which earned him Lord Ellenborough's displeasure.

A general Campbell confirmed that he had met Cochrane Johnstone in Perth the previous year and had been shown the printed prospectus for Vittoria. Lord Yarmouth, Colonel of the Duke of Cumberland's Sharpshooters denied that the Dover letter was in De Berenger's hand and confirmed that De Berenger had told him he had "very nearly arranged to go out and drill the crew and marines on board the *Tonnant*." He also described his regimental uniform as consisting of a green jacket, with a crimson collar.

He was then asked a key question by a member of the jury:

Juryman: If Colonel De Berenger had appeared before your lordship in the uniform of his corps, would it have been anything extraordinary?

Lord Yarmouth: Nothing extraordinary; it would have been more military that he should do so, though I never exacted it.

The question is interesting both because it is typical of many intelligent points raised by jurymen during the trial and because it gives an indication of the way the jury was thinking: It was the colour of the uniform that was all important to Cochrane's defence.

Park then called De Berenger's alibi witnesses; his servants William and Ann Smith who testified to their master's having been at home on 21 February, John McGuire, a Chelsea ostler, who said he saw De Berenger pass by his stables on the day of the fraud, Isaac Donthorne who lived in Westminster and Henry Doyle and his wife, all three of whom testified to seeing De Berenger at Donithorne's house on the day in question.

An architect, Thomas Hopper, was called to say that two or three hundred pounds would not be an excessive payment for the work involved in planning the Vittoria gardens.

Because the defence had called witnesses, the prosecution had the right of reply under legal procedures then in force. Gurney now rose, and was once again in fine form, the sharp edge of his sarcasm undulled by frequent use. First he dispatched the contention of the sub-plotters that they were not part of the same conspiracy that was now being tried.

"Gentlemen, if there were two conspiracies, then miracles have not ceased;, for unless you can believe that a most extraordinary miracle has occurred, it is quite impossible to conceive that there were two plots."

The three main agents, said Gurney, still had to answer for the fact that, of the day of the fraud, they sold a balance which, reduced to Consols, amounted to £1,670,000. "On this Monday the 21st, all the three have this immense quantity of stock upon their hands; they had no means of getting rid of it, for Mr. Baily has told you that but for this fraudulent transaction, it would have been impossible to have got rid of it, but at a great loss.

They had been buying as a person must do, to keep up the market, to redeem himself from loss; and on this memorable day, all this stock is sold, it is sold at a profit of upwards of ten thousand pounds; and if it had been sold without a profit of a single farthing, still the getting out without a great loss was to them very great gain. Recollect gentlemen, that just one month afterwards came the news of the rupture of the negotiation at Chatillon[7] when the premium on Omnium fell from 28 to 12 per cent; if that news had come instead of this false news, on the morning of the 21st February, the loss of these three defendants would have been upwards of one hundred and sixty thousand pounds."

Turning to the all-important question of the identity of De Berenger and the question of handwriting, Gurney told the jury that it was a subject on which they had sat through two hours of evidence which had "nauseated every man in court". The evidence of an alibi which no man living could believe.

"My learned friend, Mr. Park, last night told us we should have the evidence of two watermen who had rowed De Berenger across the Thames, who knew his person perfectly well, because it was the first Sunday after the frost had broken, and the river became navigable. I suppose the river is frozen again this morning as they are not here."[8]

The case against De Berenger was, said Gurney, alibi-proof because he had been taken up like a bale of goods at Dover and delivered from hand to hand to Lord Cochrane's house.

On Cochrane's affidavit, Gurney spoke again at length. The defence had wasted precious hours, he said, calling witnesses to confirm that which needed no confirmation; about applications to the Admiralty and so forth. But they had failed to provide confirmation of the part of the case vital to Cochrane, namely the colour of De Berenger's uniform. Cochrane put him in a green uniform, yet the prosecution had proved him to have travelled from Dover in a uniform that was red.

Serjeant Best, he said, had felt the strength of the evidence and had tried to answer it by the strange observation that Cochrane described his vistor's dress as being the green uniform he was accustomed to see him wear. "Now, " said Gurney, "if I wanted to show how it was impossible for a man to make a mistake as to the colour of the dress in which he had seen another, I should select the instance in which he had seen that other in a peculiar dress but for once."

Gurney now put his finger on two apparently very damning pieces of evidence. Why, he asked, was Cochrane's servant, Thomas Dewman, not asked what colour De Berenger's uniform was? And further, a maidservant at Green Street saw De Berenger; why was she not called? Another former servant – Isaac Davis – had been on the premises when De Berenger called and he it seemed had been sent away to serve with Admiral Cochrane in the West Indies. Was that not a suspicious circumstance? How was it he was allowed to go unless his absence was wanted more than his presence?

Secondly, Gurney picked up something that Thomas Dewman had said on the stand, that after his first, fruitless, expedition to find his master at Cumberland street, he handed the note back to De Berenger who wrote on it two or three more lines. How could this be reconciled with Cochrane's affidavit statement that he could not read the signature at the bottom of the note because it was so cramped, if there was room enough after it to add a postcript?

He next ran through the banknote evidence again, heaping scorn on the story of the planning of Vittoria – "an acre of ground behind Mr. Cochrane Johnstone's house" – and reiterated that the notes found on De Berenger were traced to all three main defendants.

"De Berenger is Du Bourg. When De Berenger is Du Bourg, the rest all follows."

The Lord Chief Justice now summed up. His address to the jury showed that he had no doubt as to the guilt of innocence of the defendants. After outlining the nature of a conspiracy charge, Lord Ellenborough went once more through the bones of the plot and then turned his attention to the principal defendant. On his part in the fraud, Ellenborough was emphatic.

"You will not, I think, have any doubt that De Berenger was the man who appeared under the name of Du Bourg; but in order to obviate or remove the impression from your minds, the learned counsel for the defendant, De Berenger did adventure or rather was forced upon an attempt, which I own it seemed to me to require the utmost firmness to attempt to execute, for there never was evidence given since I have been present in a court of justice, which carried to my mind such entire conviction of the truth and authenticity of that part of the story. "

Ellenborough then attacked De Berenger's alibi witnesses, especially Isaac Donithorne whom he described as an "inferior cabinet maker employed by Mr. Cochrane Johnstone". After running through the evidence of those who saw Du Bourg on the Dover Road, he then turned to Cochrane's affidavit and the matter of the uniform.

And at this point he consciously or unconsciously introduced a subtle distortion of the evidence as though to pre-empt a possibility which might have been forming in the jury's minds. In rehearsing the evidence of William Crane, the cab driver who took De Berenger to Green Street, he quoted Crane as saying that his fare carried a sword and a small portmanteau. In fact Crane had said that De Berenger carried a small leather portmanteau "big enough to wrap a coat up in".

Now, of the affidavit, the judge observed that De Berenger's uniform when he appeared before Cochrane must have been the red uniform in which he committed the fraud because, "it does not appear that he had any means of shifting himself." And if De Berenger presented himself to Lord Cochrane in an aide de camp's uniform, how could Cochrane reconcile his duties as an M.P. and his character as an officer and a nobleman with the act of giving him a change of clothes?

Pressing the point fully home, Ellenborough observed that assisting a man to get rid of a disguise in which he has just committed a crime "seems wholly inconsistent with the conduct of an innocent and honest man, for if he (De Berenger) appeared in such an habit, he must have appeared to any rational person fully blazoned in the costume of that or some other crime."

Before sending the jury off to consider their verdict, Ellenborough directed them to find the defendants not guilty of the first two counts of the indictment since they alleged "facts and motives in which they cannot all be supposed to be joined." An exchange between the judge and a juror at this point shows that there existed some confusion in the jury's minds over the kind of verdict they could bring in.

Juryman: They are guilty or not guilty of a conspiracy?

Ellenborough: Yes; a conspiracy, which is a crime that cannot be committed by one; it must be committed by more than one.

At 10 minutes past 6 in the evening, the jury retired and were out for two and a half hours. At 8:40 they returned their verdict – one of guilty on all defendants.

CHAPTER SIX
Candidate in Custody

"The fatal error of persons in fear of drowning is that they hold their arms up and out of the water, screaming mostly all the while."

Charles Random De Berenger "Helps and Hints, How to Protect Life, Property &tc."

When told of the court's verdict, Cochrane was stunned: a paralysis which passed rapidly into a frenzy of over-reaction. From his posture of cool disdain for the proceedings against him, he swung violently in the opposite direction and began frantically collecting new evidence, taking depositions and making ready his case for appeal.

When Cochrane finally got into court, though, a heavy psychological blow awaited him. On the Tuesday after the trial, 14 June, he appeared before the full Court of King's Bench, on which sat Lord Ellenborough and Justices Le Blanc, Bayley and Dampier.

Representing himself, without counsel, he attempted to introduce new evidence and secure a fresh trial. The judges stopped him, however, on the grounds that they couldn't hear his application because all the defendants were not present in court – McRae and Cochrane Johnstone having skipped. It was a well-established rule of court procedure, said Lord Ellenborough, which the court had already applied to another case that very morning.

Cochrane protested, "My Lords, I have now in my hands several affidavits that will prove my innocence if the court will hear them." But the judges turned him down, pointing out that if they departed from established practice for Cochrane, people would quite rightly say that there was one law for the rich and another for the poor. The following Monday, 20 June, the prosecution moved for judgement and Cochrane, De Berenger and Butt were once again before the full court. This time the judges were able to listen to applications for a new trial but first they heard counsel for Butt and De Berenger move in arrest of judgement. Serjeant Best tried to have the conviction quashed by raising a number of technicalities.

One of the legal loopholes that he tried to wriggle through was that the indictment alleged a conspiracy not against specified individuals but against the public at large. He was unsuccessful on this point but the arguments it provoked and the judges' opinions established the precedent in law that such a conspiracy was every bit as criminal as one against a named person.

Once the formal legal ritual of argument and counter argument was dispensed with, the court heard Cochrane.

In a prepared address remarkable for its eloquence and conciseness, Cochrane ran through the evidence given against him, rebutting it point by point; the banknotes, the uniform and all. "What supposition short of my absolute insanity," he asked passionately, "will account for my having voluntarily made the affidavit that has been so much canvassed, if I really knew the plot in which De Berenger appears to have been engaged?"

It had been his misfortune, Cochrane told them, to be apparently implicated with others with whom he had never had any connection except through innocent transactions. "I had met Mr. De Berenger in public company, he explained to Lord Ellenborough, "but was on no terms of intimacy with him. With Mr. Cochrane Johnstone I had the intercourse natural between such near relatives. Mr. Butt had voluntarily offered, without any reward, to carry on stock transactions, in which thousands as well as myself were engaged, in the face of day, without the smallest imputation of anything incorrect. The other four defendants were wholly unknown to me, nor have I ever directly or indirectly held any communication with them.

Of Mr. De Berenger's concern in the fraud, I have no information, except such as arises out of the late trial. With regard to Mr. Johnstone and Mr. Butt, I am willing to hope that they are guiltless. They repeatedly protested to me their innocence."

He ended his plea equally vehemently. The artifices which have been used to excite so much prejudice against me I unfeignedly despise, in spite of the injury they have done me. I know it must subside, and I look forward to justice being rendered my character sooner or later."

"I cannot feel disgraced while I know that I am guiltless. Under the influence of this sentiment, I persist in the defence of my character. I have often been in a situation where I had an opportunity of showing it. This is the first time, thank God, that I was ever called upon to defend it."

Cochrane then read out an affidavit in which he affirmed on oath the truth of his deposition of 11 March and added one or two more details (such as denying any knowledge of Holloway, McRae, Sandom or Lyte). He then attempted to introduce depositions from his servants but these were ruled inadmissable on the grounds that the witnesses themselves had been available at the time of the trial.

"It is a settled rule," said Mr. Justice Bayley, "not to allow affidavits of persons who might have been called upon the trial, much less of persons who were called." To which Lord Ellenborough added, "it would be a very dangerous thing if persons whose evidence may have been discreetly kept back, should afterwards be admitted to come forward as witnesses."

Cochrane was allowed, though, to introduce an affidavit from his brother confirming that he was ill in France and a medical certificate from the regimental surgeon.

These were dismissed by Ellenborough because they did not confirm that Cochrane knew of his brother's illness when he received the note from De Berenger at King's factory and Cochrane did not produce the letter which he claimed to have received from his brother before the data of the fraud.

Henry Cecil[9] regards the introduction of evidence of "illness" at this stage as suspicious since in the first affidavit, Cochrane spoke of his fears that an "accident" might have befallen his brother. The difference is not suspicious if Cochrane's anxiety was for the fate of a sick man who remained on the field of battle. But even if Cochrane did latch on to a "fortuitous" illness – quite a coincidence in itself – it is still not indicative of his guilt, any more than of his desperation to prove his innocence.

An affidavit was read by De Berenger's counsel setting out his service record as a volunteer officer and re-iterating the losses sustained by his family as a result of the American revolution, which he hoped would be taken into account by the court in mitigation, along with the fact that he had already spent two months in Newgate.

Richard Butt gave no instructions to his counsel but launched in person on a plea for a new trial. He affirmed his innocence of the charge, denied any intimacy with De Berenger or the minor conspirators, and added, "I can only, my Lords, accuse myself of one fault, that of being too generous and unguarded upon money affairs. Whatever your Lordships' decision may be respecting myself, I shall bow with submission, feeling conscious of my innocence of the charge upon which I have been found guilty."

None of this cut any ice with prosecutor Gurney who clung doggedly to the cloak of guilt that he had hung about the defendants' shoulders and which he was determined should remain there. The attempts of De Berenger, Cochrane and Cochrane Johnstone to defeat public justice, said Gurney, had aggravated their cases and were as absurd as they were wicked. "All the swearing before the trial, all the swearing at the trial, and all the swearing today, has proceeded on the presumption that if men will have the hardihood to swear, there will be found those who will have the credulity to believe."

In this view the judges concurred, for the applications for new trials were rejected, and the next day Mr. Justice Le Blanc pronounced sentence on the defendants.

Butt and Cochrane were ordered to pay a fine of £1,000 each to the Crown while Holloway was fined £500. All six were sentenced to serve a year in the Marshalsea prison and in addition, Butt, Cochrane and De Berenger were to be pilloried in the City, opposite the Royal Exchange.

The sentence was a stiff one and contained a deterrent element: the outcome had been eagerly awaited by the public and the bench realised that it had to act decisively to put a stop to stockjobbing frauds and restore the confidence of investors.

But if prison and the pillory were bad enough, worse was to follow for Cochrane. The Admiralty, reacting to the verdict with haste, immediately dismissed him from the service and soon after he was deprived of his Order of the Bath, his banner being unceremoniously kicked down the steps of Westminster Abbey in a "chivalrous game of football." On 5 July the question of his Parliamentary status came up in the House and the Speaker directed that Cochrane be brought from prison to take his place.

A similar attempt was made to summon Cochrane Johnstone to account, but some Members pointed out that he had been last seen at Calais some three weeks earlier.

Given the opportunity to defend himself within the privileged walls of the House, Cochrane read a speech violently attacking the whole proceedings against him; the court, the Stock Exchange, the Admiralty, and the Lord Chief Justice.

His language was apparently more suited to the quarterdeck than the debating chamber and the Speaker intervened to warn him that the House could not suffer virulent invectives or words to be made use of by him, which were not fit to be heard if not proved, adding that the House would not allow them to be repeated afterwards simply because they had been said.

Lord Castlereagh, too, warned reporters that if they repeated Cochrane's accusations in print they would be laying themselves open to libel actions. Cochrane continued his attack nevertheless and Hansard's record as a result consists largely of asterisks.

He ended with an impassioned plea for his case to be considered by a select committee, re-asserted his innocence and attributed his downfall to official collusion, particularly between the Lord Chief Justice and the Admiralty.

The House then divided on a resolution calling for his dismissal from Parliament, a resolution carried by 140 to 44. Cochrane Johnstone, too, was expelled.

A curious sideshow now took place as Henry Brougham, one of Cochrane's counsel at the trial and later Lord Chancellor, who was without a seat in Parliament, began an intrigue to get himself adopted as the candidate for Westminster. After the trial he attended a banquet given for the Friends of Parliamentary Reform and took the opportunity to fly a kite for his candidacy.

Brougham's support for Cochrane wavered as the prize of Westminster beckoned and he wrote privately to Lord Grey hinting at Cochrane's guilt saying the defence counsel had had "too good reasons" for not calling the servants from Green Street to testify. Later, when he had risen in the legal profession, he reverted to belief in Cochrane's innocence and it was when he became Lord Chancellor under William IV that he advised the Crown to give Cochrane a free pardon.

His ambitions for Westminster, though, were frustrated by the electorate who wanted back their naval hero. Sir Francis Burdett championed Cochrane from the moment of his conviction. At a large public meeting in Palace Yard, Westminster, convened to consider nominations for the vacant seat, Burdett told the electors that the question was "whether an innocent individual should be destroyed by the machinations of corruption and power".

Referring to Cochrane's defence in the House he said, "Lord Castlereagh, the nose-leader of that illustrious and august body, not having the power to gag Cochrane in the House of Commons, knowing the effect that Cochrane's speech would produce outside the House, rose in all the blushing honour of his blue ribbon to impose silence upon the corrupt and degraded press that is still suffered to exist." After attacking the conviction, Burdett declared that if Cochrane was to stand in the pillory, he would feel it his duty to stand with him.

The meeting passed resolutions declaring its belief in Cochrane's innocence and his fitness to stand as a candidate for re-election. On the hustings a few days later, Burdett proposed him and he was unanimously re-elected for Westminster. Shortly after Cochrane's re-admission to Parliament, Lord Ebrington – one of the 44 who voted against his expulsion – moved in the House that the pillory part of the sentence be remitted.

The motion stemmed from a tide of popular feeling against the Government which in turn foresaw the real possibility of street rioting if Burdett carried out his threat to join Cochrane in the pillory, and Castlereagh blandly announced that the Crown had "already decided" to remit the pillory. The decision had implications beyond Cochrane's case because, shortly after, this form of punishment was abolished altogether except for a few serious crimes.

While in prison, Cochrane busied himself preparing a pamphlet, attempting to vindicate himself and going into the charges against him in great detail. This he published early in 1815 as an open letter to Lord Ellenborough.

The pamphlet is closely reasoned and vitriolic in style, Cochrane at his most eloquently acid, and charges the Lord Chief Justice with malicious partiality in the conduct of the trial.

Cochrane quotes the Attorney-General as admitting that Ellenborough revised the short-hand note of the trial taken by William Gurney (brother, incidentally, of the prosecuting counsel) before publication, and claims that the judge's summing up in court actually asserted Cochrane's guilt, without the qualifications which appeared in the printed version.

Cochrane's object was to place on record a full statement of his defence in support of his accusations against the trial judge, whom he depicted as the arch-villain of the corrupt establishment which had framed him. The letter to Lord Ellenborough caused something of a stir but no positive action and Cochrane decided that the time was ripe for one of his grand gestures.

He had solved his previous clash with the law – in Malta – by escaping from jail and now concluded that the same device would serve very nicely to publicise his case. After serving nine months of his sentence, he escaped from Marshalsea prison on the night of 6 March 1815 by means of a rope smuggled into his cell by his servant.

He climbed from his top-floor window onto the roof tops and scaled the outer wall by lassoing the spikes placed there to prevent escape. He then drove down to his house in Hampshire and rested up for a few days waiting for a more propitious moment to capture the headlines – at present otherwise occupied with the rather more newsworthy escape of Napoleon from Elba, and the passage of the Corn Bill.

A hue and cry was raised after him and three hundred guineas reward offered for his capture, while the daily papers quarrelled among themselves about whether he was hiding in Hastings, the Channel Islands, or William Cobbett's house.

Three days later he wrote to the Speaker of the House requesting him to inform Members that "it is my intention on an early day to present myself for the purpose of taking my seat, and moving for an enquiry into the conduct of Lord Ellenborough."

On 20 March, he carried out his threat and walked boldly into the Commons where he was intercepted by a posse of Bow Street Runners. After a short struggle he was carried back to the Marshalsea and deposited in a strong room without windows, furniture or heating, and next to a cesspool. He was told by the prison authorities that if he paid his £1,000 fine and gave his word not to escape again he would be transferred to a more comfortable room, to which he replied that he would promise only that, if he escaped again, he would go straight to the House of Commons and nowhere else, and thus remained in solitary confinement.

After a month of this he wrote an address to his constituents describing his treatment and two doctors were sent to the prison to examine him. They certified him to be on the verge of typhoid as a result of the conditions in his cell and two days after he published these certificates he was moved to another room. When his sentence was up in June he was told that he would be released on payment of his fine, but he refused to pay and was kept in prison.

His friends and the prison authorities implored him not to ruin his health through his own stubborness and eventually he paid the fine by means of a £1,000 note which he endorsed on the back;

"My health having suffered by long and close confinement, and my oppressors being resolved to deprive me of property or life, I submit to robbery to protect myself from murder, in the hope that I shall live to bring the delinquents to justice."

After his release on 3 July 1815, he resumed his seat in the House and three days later gave notice that early in the next session he intended to move for the appointment of a committee of enquiry into the conduct of Lord Ellenborough. In March the following year he presented thirteen Articles of Charge of "partiality, misrepresentation, injustice and oppression" against the Lord Chief Justice.

His articles accused the judge, amongst other things, of compelling the defence to begin at midnight when they were fatigued, of confusing the cases of the various defendants, of wrongly insinuating that Cochrane was connected to De Berenger by banknotes, of devising unwarrantable objections to Cochrane's declaration that he had received a letter from his brother telling him he was ill, and of unwarrantably and repeatedly conveying the opinion that De Berenger appeared before Cochrane in the red coat and decorations in which he had committed the fraud.

Cochrane proposed and Sir Francis Burdett seconded that the charges be referred to a committee of the whole House, but when the House divided after a debate, the voting was 89 to 0 against – Cochrane and Burdett acting as tellers. The Government benches then moved that the proceedings be expunged.

Towards the end of 1815, Cochrane had been tried at Guildford for escaping from the Marshalsea prison, found guilty and ordered to pay a fine of £100. This he again refused to pay and so shortly after his attempted impeachment of Ellenborough failed, he was arrested and imprisoned once more. From this incarceration he was rescued by his Westminster constituents who raised the fine by a penny subscription.

Meanwhile, Richard Butt and Charles De Berenger had been faring little better. When Butt's sentence was up, he calmly walked out of the Marhsalsea prison without paying his £1,000 fine. He was quickly re-arrested and held until he had discharged the fine.

He then took ship for the West Indies, attempting unsuccessfully to track down the fugitive Cochrane Johnstone who, he claimed, owed him money from their former dealings. Back in England in 1817, he began a campaign for restitution of the money put into trust by the Stock Exchange and finally went too far when he placarded the streets of Westminster accusing Lord Ellenborough of pocketing the £1,000 fine. He had come to this remarkable conclusion when he discovered that both Ellenborough and the Master of the Crown Office had accounts at the same bank.

The Government prosecuted Butt for libel on the Lord Chief Justice, and he got another 15 months imprisonment for his pains.

De Berenger emerged from jail penniless and no better off for his part in the fraud but hit upon the idea of writing his memoirs as a means of restoring his fortunes. In 1816 he published a book entitled *The Noble Stockjobber* in which he claimed Cochrane was a party to the fraud.

Some of this book undoubtedly is true, but the difficulty is in knowing which parts. His assertions about Cochrane are highly suspect because the two men practically came to blows during their imprisonment together and, more importantly, because De Berenger had nothing to lose by implicating Cochrane (since they had both already been convicted of the crime) and a good deal to gain by adding a little spice to his confessions, in the tangible and gratifying form of additional book sales.

The Cochrane faction responded with a pamphlet of their own called *De Berenger Detected*, scarcely less scurrilous than the work it was intended to answer, and neither book sheds any real light on an affair already obscured by charge and counter-charge.

CHAPTER SEVEN
Question of Evidence

"Before you determine upon indulging your inclination in any manner, probe by the most serious consideration, and under the guidance of impartiality, conscience and truth, the consequences likely to result from such an indulgence."

Charles Random De Berenger "Helps and Hints, How to Protect Life, Property &tc."

The events of February and June 1814, and the long disputed question of Cochrane's guilt or innocence, involve several distinct but inter-related bones of contention.

Cochrane himself alleged that the whole affair was a politically motivated plot to get him: that the trial was rigged by the Stock Exchange and the Government – particularly the Admiralty – that perjured testimony was given against him, that his own case was badly got-up and departed from his instructions, and above all that the judge was biased in his conduct of the case.

Then there is the evidence itself: Cochrane's knowledge of De Berenger, the tracing of banknotes, his stock dealings, and the thorny question of the colour of De Berenger's uniform.

It must be said at the outset that there is no direct evidence for a plot to get something on Cochrane. It is fair to add that one would not expect such evidence to exist even if there had been a plot of this kind.

There are several circumstances which do suggest a certain element of collusion. Soon after the fraud, on 2 March, the subcommittee offered the job of representing the Stock Exchange in any legal steps it might take, to Ralph Sandom's attorney, Highmore, as an inducement to him to persuade Sandom to confess.

This indicates that, at that stage, the subcommittee had no legal representative. Five days later, on 7 March, they met Lord Melville, First Lord of the Admiralty. What took place at the meeting is not recorded, but it seems very probable that the subcommittee was trying to get the Crown to undertake the prosecution on the grounds that part of the conspiracy involved false dispatches to the Admiralty.

Having got little tangible support from the Home Secretary two days earlier, Charles Laurence decided to try to enlist the help of Melville. But the Stock Exchange got no further with the Admiralty than they had with the Home Office except for the rather vague promise that they "might apply to the Attorney General, if they had any occasion for legal advice."

One other apparent result of this meeting, however, was that they put Germain Lavie, the Admiralty's solicitor, on their own payroll, because four days later, on 11 March, his name crops up for the first time as "solicitor to the Stock Exchange". Lavie was the man responsible for the defence of Lord Gambier at his court martial in 1809 against Cochrane's allegations over the Basque Roads affair. There was certainly no love lost between the two men, Cochrane having accused the lawyer of manufacturing charts of the Basque Roads to support Gambier's case.

The appointment of Lavie may or may not have had political undertones but it was certainly the first blow against Cochrane's case.

The Government's attitude was, in fact, one of caution and an unwillingness to become involved until there seemed the prospect of a successful prosecution: They had tangled with Cochrane and come out looking foolish too often to take any chances. Cochrane in their eyes was a wild-man – unpredictable and dangerous when cornered. Neither Sidmouth not Melville wished to risk the deluge of ridicule and abuse that Cochrane would make sure to bring down on their heads if they associated themselves with a prosecution that failed. Stock Exchange was left to shoulder the burden alone: So the to take the decision to proceed with an expensive private prosecution in an uncertain case, resting largely on circumstantial evidence.

And to their credit they did exactly what Cochrane himself would have done in the circumstances. They nailed their colours to the mast and sailed straight for the enemy.

Once they had secured a True Bill from the Grand Jury after preferring an indictment against the conspirators, the Crown then stole quietly from the wings to take over the prosecution itself.

It is true to say that Cochrane had generated sufficient mistrust and ill-feeling in Whithall for it to operate against him in a number of ways. Having made enemies of Secretary Croker, Lord Melville, and indeed the entire Government front bench in the House, he found no support forthcoming in a moment of crisis and it seems likely that Whitehall felt secretly relieved at the prospect of having him off their hands, whatever the rights and wrongs of the charges against him.

The Government also suspected that Richard Butt, in his capacity as a clerk in the Navy Office, and later from his contacts there, was the source supplying Cochrane and Sir Francis Burdett with much of the ammunition for their Parliamentary attacks on corruption and abuses. No doubt they felt that a successful prosecution of both men would seal the leak.

Whatever the Government's attitude to the prosecution, there is some evidence that the Stock Exchange specifically wished to have Cochrane convicted. In its instructions to Lavie, the subcommittee noted (after describing the part played by McRae, Sandom, Holloway and Lyte) "the only thing we have to add on the part of this minor plot is to repeat the caution not to make it too prominent lest it should have the effect of obtaining the acquittal of the only real object of this prosecution, Viz, Lord Cochrane Mr. Cochrane Johnstone and Mr. Butt. If Vinn were to be put forward in the front of the battle we fear it might have this effect."

As to the getting up of his case and the conduct of the prosecution, Cochrane certainly had some legitimate cause for grievance – although as happened so frequently, he ruined his chances of getting sympathy and some redress by bending the facts to suit himself and overstating his case.

One of his chief complaints was that the barrister who drew up his March 11 affidavit, naming De Berenger, and to whom he confided details of his case was none other than the man who subsequently appeared at the trial leading the prosecution, John Gurney.

This claim was later demolished in the *Law Magazine and Review* by Gurney's son, Russell Gurney, who quoted Cochrane contradicting himself on the occasion of moving for a new trial, when he said that he "without any communication whatsoever with any other person, and without assistance, on the impulse of the moment, prepared the . . . affidavit."

The real strength of Cochrane's claim, said Russell Gurney, was that on 2 April (after the publication of the affidavit) Cochrane consulted Gurney on what legal action he could take against the Stock Exchange to vindicate his character. The material given to Gurney for consideration was "almost exclusively reports and affidavits which had already been published, and gave no information which could be used in any way prejudicial to Lord Cochrane."

Because of the thoroughness of this rebuttal out of Cochrane's own mouth, the *Law Magazine* saw fit to reverse its position of support for Cochrane's innocence to one of wishing that they could "come to another conclusion upon the evidence and believe that Lord Cochrane was as entirely innocent as he so frequently and vehemently protested he was."

It is a great pity that the *Law Magazine* allowed itself to be persuaded so easily. here is no doubt that Cochrane was, in the words of the magazine, "by no means careful of facts", but the fact remains that whether Cochrane consulted Gurney over a possible libel action against the Stock Exchange, or over the affidavit, he still revealed all the details of his case, and what is more, Gurney suggested to him a line of defence against the allegations that he was mixed up with De Berenger.

This is made clear by the subcommittee's own records. Referring to the question of Du Bourg's uniform, they minuted,

" . . . it is possible that there might have been a green coat in the portmanteau and that De Berenger changed it for his scarlet coat while he was waiting in Lord Cochrane's room. This idea we know 'vas suggested to Lord Cochrane by one of the legal advisers he first consulted."

This could only be a reference to Gurney, and presumably the information could only have come from Gurney, who was by now under a retainer from the Stock Exchange.

In his letter to the *Law Magazine*, Russell Gurney also repeated another error which was in many respects as crucial to Cochrane's case as the colour of the uniform: that it appeared from the report of the subcommittee that five days before publication of Cochrane's affidavit naming De Berenger, the subcommittee already had De Berenger's name from an informant and that a warrant had been obtained for his arrest. Neither of these statements is correct.

The facts are that on March 8, three days before Cochrane drew up his affidavit, William Harrison gave De Berenger's name to the subcommittee. The information was not acted upon until March 11, when they considered applying for a writ of *habeus corpus* but did not do so.

The date of issue of the warrant for De Berenger's arrest was given by Joseph Wood, the Alien Office agent at the trial. It was March 17, five days after Cochrane's affidavit was published.

Getting Gurney for the prosecution two or three days after he had been consulted by Cochrane, was a shrewd move on the part of Germain Lavie, whether intentional or not. Not only did the Stock Exchange get the services of one of the most able and sought-after barristers of the day but also one who knew what Cochrane's defence would most probably be, and this might explain the extraordinary defence that his own counsel decided to put forward at the trial – that Cochrane had mistaken the colour of the uniform.

This was certainly contrary to his instructions, and obviously took Gurney by surprise because he several times posed prepared questions which could be aimed only at breaking down a defence based on Cochrane's assertion of having seen a green uniform. (For example, when he asked, why was Cochrane's servant, Thomas Dewman, not questioned about the colour of De Berenger's uniform while he was on the stand? Clearly if the defence admits that the uniform really was the false red one, then such questions are irrelevant.)

The reasons for his counsel not calling the servants and for venturing the "mistake" theory are examined in more detail later, but whatever the reasons, Cochrane was furious and henceforward continued to insist that there had been no mistake: De Berenger's uniform had been green.

If the defence was generally inept, the prosecution was ruthless. One example of how the prosecution stage-managed the trial concerns the Dover letter – the dispatch that De Berenger, as Du Bourg, sent from Dover to Admiral Foley.

A good deal of evidence was called at the trial to show that this letter was in De Berenger's handwriting. Germain Lavie himself took the stand as the chief prosecution witness to testify that the letter was in the defendant's hand, since Timothy Wright, landlord of the Ship Inn Hotel was indisposed and could not appear.

What would Wright have testified had he been well enough to do so? He would have told the court what he had already told the Stock Exchange and what they in turn had told Gurney: that the watermark of the Dover letter did not match that of the stationery kept at the Ship. In other words, that De Berenger only pretended to write a letter and the document sent to Admiral Foley had been brought ready written.

This does not, of course, rule out De Berenger's having written it, but it does mean that there is no obvious evidence to suggest that he did or to justify the force with which his handwriting was sworn to. And moreover, there is some evidence that his English was not perfectly fluent. He apologises in The Noble Stockjobber – a rambling work – for his "repeated encroachments on his indulging reader's patience, on the ground that he is writing in what to him is a foreign language".

Gurney overstepped the mark in many ways during the trial. He casually distorted facts to suit his case, as for example when he said that the defendants had bought the large quantity of stock they sold, only a week or two before. The Stock Exchange must have known, and Gurney must have known that they had all been speculators for a long time – especially Butt who was, in effect, a freelance broker.

He also perpetuated claims in his closing address which he had not proved by testimony. He said for example that even if the defendants could have sold their stock without any profit at all it was still a great gain to them because they ran the risk of making an enormous loss. Just a month later, said Gurney, Omnium fell from 28 to 12 and they would have lost upwards of £160,000. In fact, had Gurney consulted the Times for 23 February (the settlement day when the accused would have had to sell their stock if there had been no fraud) he would have seen that far from falling, Omnium was actually rising in expectation of victory and stood at 27½.

Cochrane's main criticism of the trial concerned its conduct by Lord Ellenborough. The judge, he said, was biased, and inconsistencies in the prosecution case were repeated with some conviction by the judge in his summing up without having been proved in court.

In many criminal trials, the cases of both the prosecution and defence are internally inconsistent or illogical. To take an example from this case, it was the prosecution's intention to show on one hand that De Berenger was on intimate terms with Lord Cochrane (in order to re-inforce suspicion of conspiracy) and on the other that De Berenger was no more than a casual acquaintance (so that it should seem incredible that he would appear before Cochrane in his sharpshooter's uniform while still under the Rules of the King's Bench).)

This kind of inconsistency – though it is the delight of the thriller-writer – really means nothing at all. Where evidence is purely circumstantial it is impossible for the prosecution to present the jury with certain knowledge of a crime as if it were known directly. Instead the prosecution must build a case; must outline a picture to the jury of how it is convinced events must have occurred, and convey its conviction on this point by whatever legitimate devices it can. Similarly, the defence cannot rebut the implications of a chain of circumstantial evidence except by attempting to show that the picture painted by the prosecution does not carry the certainty it is intended to convey.

If, for example, the wife of a poisoned man is proved to have bought arsenic shortly before his death, then the act is beyond dispute. What is in dispute is the interpretation of the act. Was it – as the prosecution alleges – a prelude to murder? Or was it – as the defence patiently explains – merely to get rid of the rats in the cellar? Nothing in law compels either prosecution or defence to be logical or consistent in presenting their version of the facts: the only test is whether they are successful in convincing a judge and jury.

In the case of Lord Cochrane, the judge, Lord Ellenborough, was so much convinced of the accuracy of the prosecution picture that on occasions he even added a little of the detail himself.

He interrupted the proceedings more than 250 times. On about 70 of these occasions he interrupted while witnesses were being questioned by the prosecuting counsel. While the same witnesses were being examined by the defence, he intervened more than 180 times. In other words, he felt in necessary to break in on defence questioning two and a half times more frequently than on prosecution questioning. Any attempt to measure the number of occasions on which these interruptions were favourable to the defence and on which they were favourable to the prosecution must necessarily be largely subjective. But on any reading, the latter outweigh the former by a wide margin.

Examples of Ellenborough's prompting of prosecution witnesses and impeding the defence are so numerous that it is difficult to choose merely representative samples. Germain Lavie's testimony is perhaps illuminating because it shows such clear bias for the witness and against defence counsel. Lavie was called on, as noted above, to testify that the Dover letter was in De Berenger's handwriting.

Defence counsel Park had his first skirmish with the judge over whether Lavie should be permitted to testify that when he first saw the letter before the trial he said that he believed it was De Berenger's hand.

Objecting to this attempt to introduce hearsay evidence, Park retorted: "you know as well as any man that what you said to anybody is no evidence."

Ellenborough intervened to say: "it is a measure strongly indicative of his persuasion, it is an act accompanying his seeing it."

Having thus admitted evidence of a type which was then, and is today, inadmissable, Ellenborough next upbraided Park for asking the question, "Was Mr Stevens applied to?" (for further evidence of identification). Lavie prevaricated at this, and went off at a tangent until Park stopped him, saying, "That is not my question."

At this Ellenborough told the defence counsel, "Put your question more distinctly."

It is hard to imagine how the question "Was Mr. Stevens applied to?" could be put more distinctly.

Most interesting of all is to compare the result of Lavie's asserting "I verily believe it to be his handwriting", with the judge's reaction to the reply of De Berenger's solicitor, Gabriel Tahourdin, who had known him for many years.

Asked if the Dover letter was in De Berenger's hand, he replied, "certainly not." Lord Ellenborough here interrupted to warn the witness, "be upon your guard."

When Tahourdin continued to assert that he had seen De berenger's letters a thousand times and that the Dover letter was not in his hand, Ellenborough sulkily replied, "the gentleman may look at the . . .. letters but that furnishes no argument for a person would certainly write a disguised hand at that time if ever he did in his life."[10]

In other words, when Lavie asserted that the letter was De Berenger's, the assertion met with Lord Ellenborough's approval. Contradictory testimony was met first by the veiled implication that the witness was lying under oath and when the witness refused to be shaken, Ellenborough's explanation was that he must be mistaken because De Berenger had disguised his hand. Whatever evidence was given, in Lord Ellenborough's mind it was proof of guilt.

Curiously enough, Lord Yarmouth when asked if the letter was in De Berenger's hand, replied in precisely the same terms as Tahourdin, "certainly not." In his case, however, he was not told to be upon his guard.

If it is accepted that cases are won or lost on the climate of certainty created by the prosecution or doubt created by the defence, then Lord Cochrane's case was lost from the start. For from the first morning, Ellenborough showed time and again that he accepted the prosecution's version of events. His impartiality extended this far: that if Cochrane could have proved his innocence he would have been acquitted.

In a case which depended on circumstantial evidence, the only answer to the charge was itself circumstantial, and since Lord Ellenborough clearly threw his weight behind the circumstances favoured by the prosecution, so did the jury.

Cochrane's other chief complaint about the trial concerned the lateness of the adjournment and the fact that Ellenborough insisted on the defence opening its case at 10 o'clock at night when the court had already been sitting for 13 hours, and letting it go on until 3 o'clock in the morning – a total of 18 hours.

Dividing the case at this time was defended by Lord Ellenborough's descendants on the grounds that long sittings were the rule at the period rather than the exception, and the rather extraordinary observation that none of the jury complained of being fatigued, as though to suggest that the whole matter was merely a technical argument and that no-one in practice was harmed by the judge's decision.

This view simply does not stand up when taken together with the fact that Park specifically complained to the judge of fatigue; that both he and Best felt compelled to apologise to the jury for the lateness of the hour (although doubtless getting as much mileage as possible out of the point) and that moreover, Thomas Hopper – the architect called to testify on Cochrane Johnstone's behalf – was actually taken ill after the long sitting and was not well enough to appear until later the following day.

Admiral Foley who had travelled up to Town for the trial, and who was constantly suffering ill-health after being wounded at Trafalgar, hence his shore job as Port Admiral at Deal, suffered a relapse immediately after the proceedings and wrote to Croker at the Admiralty, "Severe indisposition has confined me for some days to the house." He remained in London until well enough to return to Deal a week or so later.

There was indeed a great deal of merit in Lord Ellenborough's stated reason for carrying on into the small hours, that it would inconvenience Lord Melville; First Lord of the

Admiralty, Colonel Torrens; Secretary to the Commander in Chief, and Henry Goulburn; Undersecretary of State for the Colonial Office, if they were kept from pressing affairs of state for another day.

But no-one can pretend that dividing the cause at such a late hour did not have a marked effect, or that the jury were able after 18 hours to give the same attention to the defence speeches that they had given the prosecution. While long sittings may well have been common 200 years ago, and lawyers used to working long hours, there is no evidence that jurors of that date were any tougher than those of today.

Before examining Cochrane's case in more detail, it is worth looking a little more closely at the justice received by the other defendants. Of the guilt of the minor actors in the conspiracy, Holloway, Sandom, Lyte and Alexander McRae, there can be no doubt. Holloway and Lyte confessed to the Stock Exchange implicating their confederates, and Sandom was in any case recognised by the Post Boy who drove them.

The evidence against McRae was complete, and he promptly confirmed the jury's verdict by fleeing, although he was later arrested and sentenced.

The evidence of identification against De Berenger was overwhelming and his arrest while attempting to flee the country under an alias clinched the case against him as "Colonel Du Bourg". His choice of alias for the fraud also represents an interesting example of the criminal's reluctance to abandon his identity altogether and sticking to his own initials for an alias. It also saves money on having your luggage rebranded.

Cochrane Johnstone's guilt was not proved with such certainty, but the evidence was plainly sufficient to convict: his motive was clear since he was up to his ears in debt and under pressure from his creditors; he sold by far the largest quantity of stock; and he was deeply involved with De Berenger, even standing as one of his sureties as a prisoner within the Rules of the King's Bench.

Above all, his past record was that of a thoroughgoing scoundrel and after the trial he fled the country and was never heard of again. His connection with McRae was revealed through his own inept attempts to extract £10,000 from the subcommittee.

Against Richard Butt, the evidence was far from satisfactory. No connection between him and De Berenger was ever established: he had been a successful speculator for years and had made far larger profits, legitimately, on previous occasions. He was not alleged to be in any financial difficulty. The only connection between Butt and the fraud is that banknotes in De Berenger's possession had once been in Butt's hands. These, however, were paid to De Berenger by Cochrane Johnstone and came from the stock account kept quite innocently by Butt for both Cochrane and Cochrane Johnstone.

It was never proved, nor even expressly alleged, that Butt handed money over to De Berenger. On the evidence presented, Butt should definitely not have been convicted and he seems to have been a victim of his own social climbing; a casualty of his acquaintance with the Cochranes.

Cochrane's case is considerably more complex and the principal difficulty of those who have argued for his guilt is the question of motive. Ostensibly this should have been financial, but a closer inspection of his circumstances shows that this view is quite unsupportable.

To begin with, he was not – like his uncle – a penniless adventurer living on his wits. He was a highly successful naval officer who had taken tens of thousands in prize money and who owned a large country house in Hampshire and a private yacht, as well as running a large London house. He was also a successful speculator who with Butt's help had made over £4,700 in the previous five months. What is more, his prospects of further prize money from the war with America were exceedingly rosy: if he repeated only one-tenth of his previous performance, he would augment his personal fortune still further.

Above all in his favour is the fact that his standing order to his broker was to sell on a one per cent rise in the market, so that however spectacular a fraud were pulled off, it was impossible for his profits to exceed the amount he actually made – £1,700: a small sum when compared to his expectations. It was argued at his trial and repeated by later writers that he and his alleged fellow conspirators were selling under favourable conditions when false news of victory was received, and that without the stimulus of this news they stood to lose perhaps tens of thousands by depressing the market if they had to sell by settlement day, two days after the fraud. This argument is an ingenious display of mental agility because it assumes Cochrane's guilt as a necessary condition of its consequence.

Cochrane's holdings were relatively modest and were in Omnium alone. If he was unconnected with the fraud, he would have expected to dispose of them quite easily on settlement day without depressing the market sufficiently to deny him his one per cent profit.

Feeling the strength of these arguments, Lord Ellenborough's descendants and other writers have looked elsewhere for a motive, and their roving imaginations have settled on the "practical joker" theory. Cochrane, they say, was a daring fellow constantly trying his courage, pitting his wits against the odds, and given to attempts to make fools of those in authority. A hoax on the Stock Exchange was just the sort of prank that would appeal to his boyish sense of humour and his desire to ridicule the establishment – like his escapades in Malta in taking on the Prize Court and escaping from jail, not to mention his repeated impertinences to senior officers and reckless behaviour in action, and the many *ruses de guerre* he employed such as sailing under false colours.

Although superficially tempting, this line doesn't stand up to scrutiny. If Cochrane's personal history shows anything, it shows an enviable record of courage and integrity under the most difficult conditions. His activities in Malta and Parliament may well appear as merry japes when dressed up for his autobiography and read in the comfort of an armchair far from the danger of battle or the dank discomforts of a jail cell.

But they were undertaken at the time with the serious intention of righting injustices and they required no less courage and determination to carry off than his attack on the French fleet. Other radical politicans of the period went considerably further in their attacks on the establishment – Sir Francis Burdett, for example, who was consigned to the Tower for publishing a letter challenging Parliament's right to imprison one of his constituents – and these episodes, too, make amusing anecdotes after the event, just as they were turned to good use at the time by cartoonists such as Gillray.

No-one has suggested, however, that the penchant of Burdett or William Cobbett for scrapes with authority predisposed them to commit criminal acts. What is in the back of many people's minds when they are swayed by the plausibility of the "hoaxer" theory is that the fraud was the sort of crime – rather like an insurance swindle where it would be possible for the conspirators to convince themselves that no-one would be hurt except speculators who richly deserved all that they got, and also one where, because the instrument of crime was the written word rather than the club or pistol, then those involved were not faced with a clear-cut moral decision about the consequences of their actions.

There is a good deal in this argument, and it is not difficult to picture even an honourable man being drawn into what seemed on the surface no more than a practical joke with the added incentive of a little profit for no apparent risk, at the expense of City sharks.

Had Cochrane been anything but a naval officer, an element of doubt might well exist on this point. But it was Lord Ellenborough's grandson[11] who pointed out that the most serious charge on the indictment was that of attempting to deceive the Admiralty and a senior naval officer (Admiral Foley at Deal) with false news of a war at its most critical stage.

For the Captain of a battle ship of the line, on active service in time of war, to commit such an act would be among the gravest of crimes – little short of treason – and it would be impossible for an officer of Cochrane's experience to drift into such a conspiracy without fully understanding its serious consequences. This fact alone is sufficient to repel attempts to involve Cochrane by the extraordinary device of playing down the serious nature of the crime.

Cochrane's opponents clearly recognised that the more grave the charge against him, the greater the difficulty of getting anyone to believe in his guilt.

To begin with, therefore, no satisfactory motive has been established for Cochrane to participate in such a crime. Allowing for the sake of argument, though, that he might have had some secret, unknown motive, still the evidence for his complicity is extremely weak. The prosecution case, both as charged in court and as developed later by those who believe in guilt, comes to this:

Why did Cochrane buy a large amount of stock on February 11 prior to the fraud?

Why was Cochrane hanging about in London at the time of the fraud – ostensibly patenting a lantern – when he should have been superintending the fitting out of the *Tonnant?*

How did De Berenger know that Cochrane was at 13 Green Street to which Cochrane had moved only some, days before unless the two men were on intimate terms?

Why did De Berenger go to Cochrane's house?

How can Cochrane's affidavit assertion be supported that the signature on the note delivered to him at King's factory was illegible, given that De Berenger had taken the note back from the servant and added two or three more lines to it?

Why did Cochrane say that De Berenger's uniform was green when the coachmen and other witnesses testified to a red uniform?

Why did Cochrane give him a change of dress?

Why were Cochrane's servants not put on the witness stand to testify about the colour of De Berenger's uniform?

And were not some of their affidavits contradictory to the statements they first made to Cochrane's solicitors about the uniform?

Why did De Berenger have in his possession banknotes traceable to Cochrane?

And how can Cochrane's claim to be the first person to give De Berenger's name to the subcommittee be reconciled with the Stock Exchange's statement that they already had De Berenger's name, that a warrant was already out for his arrest, and that one of their informants was eventually given the reward money?

All these questions taken together constitute a formidable body of circumstances that seem to argue for Cochrane's guilt. Yet all of them can be answered perfectly satisfactorily either by evidence presented at the time of the trial, or soon after, or by evidence which has subsequently come to light, particularly from the records of the Stock Exchange.

In the first place, and as his counsel pointed out at the trial, Cochrane's buying of stocks on February 11 was in no way out of the ordinary. He had bought as large quantities before and had been speculating on margins for some months, making £4,700 between 22 October 1814 and 11 February 1814. Many other individuals bought as large sums at the same time. The buying of stock alone was in no way indicative of guilt, although it was of course a necessary antecedent to being considered a potential conspirator.

The question of why Cochrane was in London at the time of the fraud instead of supervising work on the *Tonnant*, is of some interest. The Bow Street officer employed by the Stock Exchange, Sayer, unearthed an apparently curious fact in the course of his investigations in Green Street which he reported in confidence to the subcommittee.

There was, he said, a lady "under Lord Cochrane's protection", expecting a child and lying-in at number 13. He reported this as a correction to his earlier statement that there were three or four men staying at the house. These men, he now believed, were the lady's medical attendants, or visiting relatives.

De Berenger, too, referred in his "memoirs" of the fraud to a lady being at Green Street when he called, and he also jumped to the same conclusion as Sayer about her presence. What neither Sayer, nor the subcommittee, nor De Berenger knew at the time was that the lady was in fact Cochrane's wife, Kitty Barnes, whom he had married 18 months earlier in secret because of family opposition, and who was more than seven months pregnant with their first child, Thomas Barnes. The child was born some weeks later on 18 April 1814.

Cochrane could at any time have brought this forward as a most compelling and convincing explanation of his remaining in Town for the last few weeks before sailing on a lengthy tour of duty in North America. The fact that he chose to protect his young bride rather than let her become embroiled in the affair speaks volumes on his behalf.

Moreover, as Henry Cecil has said, "it is difficult to think that Lady Cochrane did not firmly believe in her husband's innocence."[12]

One might indeed go further and say that, since she saw De Berenger on the morning of 21 February, she was very probably in a position to know that her husband was innocent.

It was also alleged at the trial that De Berenger must have been on intimate terms with Cochrane to know the address to which he had moved only days before. It is hard to see why this "must" have been so. The two individuals most deeply involved in the plot were De Berenger himself and Cochrane's uncle. It would have been perfectly natural that De Berenger should have taken the trouble to learn the address from Cochrane Johnstone, especially since he entertained the highest hopes of persuading Cochrane to take him along when the *Tonnant* sailed.

This indeed supports Cochrane's affidavit statement that De Berenger came to him for that purpose, and it is common ground that the Prussian was in urgent need of an escape route.

There is another, and far simpler possible explanation but one which unfortunately cannot be verified. Cochrane moved into Green Street on 17 February. On that 17 February he wrote to De Berenger the letter which De Berenger himself quoted in his book *The Noble Stockjobber* as part of an attempt to prove Cochrane guilty, but omitted the address from which Cochrane sent it.

Was this omission, perhaps, because Cochrane had sent it from Number 13 Green Street?

Precisely why he decided to go to Cochrane's house is a more difficult question. The prosecution's suggestion that it was because the conspirators had forgotten to provide him with a hideout for his return to London does not stand up, because De Berenger did not in fact hide out there; after changing his clothes and spending only an hour or so at the house, he went back to his lodgings. If, as also suggested, he went there simply to obtain a disguise, still the question remains whether it was to disguise his false red uniform as the coachmen's evidence suggested, and the prosecution alleged, or his green sharpshooter's uniform as Cochrane claimed. This question I shall return to presently in greater depth. Disguise or no disguise, though, there is no reason to doubt Cochrane's claim that De Berenger's primary reason for visiting him was to attempt to secure an immediate hiding place on the *Tonnant,* and passage out of the country when she sailed. America, the country of opportunity must have beckoned De Berenger strongly in the hour of his need.

And if he called on Cochrane prepared to sail, this would also confirm his assertion that he had come equipped with his green sharpshooter's uniform. For, whether or not Cochrane was party to the conspiracy, the fugitive De Berenger would still have to act the role of sharpshooter for the benefit of the crew and officers of the *Tonnant.*

What reason would De Berenger have for believing he could prevail on Cochrane to take him on board? He gives the reason himself in *The Noble Stockjobber* when he quotes the following letter, sent by Cochrane just days before the fraud:

> "Dear Sir,
> Your papers are very clear, as all writings are which come from your pen. Such, however, are the circumstances in which I am placed, that it is not in my power at present to avail myself of your polite offer. If you will go to America with me, we will talk the subject over on the passage.
> Yours very truly,
> COCHRANE.
> February 17th, 1814.
> Baron de Berenger, etc."

It is fair to add that this letter is also evidence against Cochrane's claim that he failed to recognise the handwriting of the note De Berenger sent out to King's factory.

Of this note, and his claim that the signature was illegible, the prosecution made a good deal of capital. How could the signature be illegible due to being so close to the bottom of the paper, asked the prosecutor, if De Berenger added more lines to it?

Cochrane himself pointed out in his Letter to Lord Ellenborough that the prosecutor was forgetting that there were two side to the paper, or that the addition might have been written at the top. There is also a simpler and more likely explanation of which Cochrane would have been unaware. If De Berenger, for reasons of secrecy, had decided to send out the note on its first journey to Cumberland Street unsigned, or signed only with his initials, and then, feeling a growing sense of urgency, decided to sign it before sending it out on its second trip, to Cock Lane, this would explain not only how he was able to add to an apparently already-finished note, but also why the signature was close to the bottom of the paper.

But in any case, Cochrane was a senior naval officer at whose home officers of all kinds habitually called to discuss service matters and there was nothing in any way out of the ordinary in his receiving such a note and returning home: it was a commonplace of service life.

This explanation was not accepted at the time because if Cochrane considered his lamp patent more important than supervising work on the *Tonnant*, why should he allow himself to be distracted by a scribbled note on a scrap of paper? We now know, though, that his real reason for remaining in Town was that his wife was lying-in at Green Street and the lamp patent partly a diversion for his hands, while his mind was elsewhere.

The central and most damning piece of evidence against Cochrane, and that which gave some substance to the other peripheral circumstances, was of course his claim of seeing a green uniform when the coachmen, Crane and Shilling, testified to seeing a red uniform. Here again is a case where a simple circumstance has been complicated endlessly by charge and counter-charge.

Cochrane's explanation of the discrepancy was the simple one that De Berenger had changed his uniform, either in the coach or in 13 Green Street while waiting. This, too, was the explanation which suggested itself to the Stock Exchange subcommittee, which minuted in its confidential notes, "from all the enquiry made by a deputation of the subcommittee who undertook a journey to Dover in the last month to follow up these investigations . . . they could not ascertain that De Berenger had any portmanteau with him, nor do Lord Cochrane or any of his servants make mention of it. It now however distinctly appears that he had one as Crane has before deposed. This circumstance however may assist Lord Cochrane and his servants with respect to their having sworn that the coat De Berenger had on was green, because it is possible that there might have been a green coat in the portmanteau and that De Berenger changed it for his scarlet coat while he was waiting in Lord Cochrane's room."

The evidence for this explanation is considerable. Simeon Solomon, the military outfitter from whom De Berenger bought the scarlet uniform, described to the subcommittee the bag in which his customer packed it. It was a brown leather portmanteau "about 20 inches or 2 feet long and 10 or 12 inches broad." The hackney driver, William Crane, also referred in court to the bag carried by his passenger as a "small portmanteau, big enough to wrap a coat up in", although he thought the colour was black as far as he could recollect.

And Thomas Shilling, too, testified to De Berenger's having a small portmanteau and a sword on the seat of the chaise.

The opportunity existed for De Berenger to change coats in the carriage – despite Lord Ellenborough's observation that he did not appear to have the means of shifting himself when, as the chaise driver testified, he pulled up the blind of the coach window between Lambeth Road and Marsh Gate.

An opportunity also existed for him to do so in Crane's hackney cab or at Cochrane's house while he was left alone waiting for Cochrane to return. According to witnesses at Dover, De Berenger was wearing a sword. By the time he reached London in the chaise, Shilling tells us he had removed the sword and placed it on the seat. Taking off the sword would certainly be a necessary preliminary to changing the tunic.

Above all, the question stands out, why should De Berenger travel from Dover to London with a portmanteau "big enough to wrap a coat up in" unless he actually did have a coat wrapped up in it? What else could the bag have contained? Not food, because he stopped several times to eat on the journey as part of the plan to spread false news and he carried the gold Napoleons for that purpose. Not writing materials, because he called for those at the Ship Inn and in any case brought the letter ready-written.

It is hard to believe that he journeyed with an empty portmanteau.

The difficulty in accepting this theory is that if De Berenger did take the precaution of changing from the scarlet uniform into his green Sharpshooter's coat, why should he need to borrow a hat and coat from Cochrane?

The answer to this is bound up with the testimony of William Crane, which has several interesting aspects. Despite the fact that Crane's testimony is often regarded as crucial to Cochrane's guilt, and the man himself has been alternately styled as the prosecution's star witness, and as a perjurer of the deepest dye, his evidence is curiously ambivalent. For one thing, it was he who volunteered, quite unprompted, that De Bourg's portmanteau was big enough to wrap a coat in even though he was put on the stand by the prosecution to implicate Cochrane.

For another, he was the only one of the many witnesses who got a good look at Du Bourg who failed to mention – either at his two confidential appearances before the subcommittee or in court – the prominent military star and badge on the breast of the scarlet uniform. All he ever testified to was "a red coat underneath his greatcoat", and the object of his testimony was really only to place Du Bourg on the doorstep of Cochrane's house.

Now the collar of De Berenger's sharpshooter's uniform was red in contrast to the bottle-green of the jacket. And Crane got a good look at his passenger only when he left the cab at Green Street, since De Berenger transferred directly from one coach to another, door-to-door, at the Marsh Gate. It is perfectly possible, therefore, that when he testified to a red jacket, Crane was reporting an inference drawn from seeing a red collar under a buttoned greatcoat: an inference re-inforced by comparing notes with the other witnesses.

This speculation has the defect of being incapable of verification, but it also has the merit of fitting all the facts and at the same time not requiring the invention of a villainous character either for Crane himself or for Cochrane. Moreover, it also explains why De Berenger would feel the need of a disguise after his plan to escape on board the *Tonnant* had failed, because he would have believed himself to have been compromised even in his proper uniform through being spotted by Crane.

This, indeed, is a far more probable explanation of De Berenger's behaviour than that in which he travels all the way to London dressed in his impostor's uniform, carrying an empty portmanteau, and resorts to the house of one of the most famous men in England for a coat two sizes too large with which to disguise himself.

The objection has still been raised, though, why should Cochrane accede to De Berenger's request for a change of clothes unless De Berenger was in a position to demand a disguise by reason of their mutual self-interest in covering up the fraud? This objection stems on one hand from a misunderstanding created by Cochrane's defence counsel at the trial (probably on his own initiative, since he also took it upon himself to advance the "mistake" theory over the colour) and from a misreading of the evidence. De Berenger did not demand a change of clothes: In fact, he merely asked for the loan of a hat and it was Cochrane who volunteered the coat.

In his March 11 affidavit he says De Berenger told him, "under present circumstances, however, he must use a great liberty, and request the favour of me to lend him a hat to wear instead of his military cap. I gave him one which was in a back room with some things that had not been packed up, and having tried it on, his uniform appeared under his greatcoat;I therefore offered him a black coat that was laying on a chair, and which I did not intend to take with me."

Surely, it would be an insane act for Cochrane to admit to *offering* the coat if he was party to the fraud, when it would have been so easy to say that De Berenger asked for it? If he was a conspirator he would have been announcing his guilt to the world by publishing the fact that he volunteered a disguise to the phoney Du Bourg.

If, as the evidence appears to indicate, De Berenger changed into his sharpshooter's uniform in the coach, then not only might Crane have seen a red collar and inferred a red uniform, but so too might the manservant, Thomas Dewman, who opened the door to him and any other servant present at the time.

And, in fact, at their preliminary examination by Cochrane's solicitors, that is precisely what some of them said. At this stage, the evidence was not by itself damaging to Cochrane because uneducated servants could not be blamed for not knowing the colour-scheme of a particular regimental uniform.

Cochrane, though, seems to have become panicky at the prospect of a competent prosecuting counsel turning a red collar into a red tunic, or an "it-might-have-been-red" tunic, under cross-examination. And he probably "helped them to remember" that the uniform was green when they came to draw up their depositions.

Like many accused persons before and since who have an answer to the charge but who feel that their story, though true, sounds somewhat unconvincing in places, he decided to improve it a little. In the words of Henry Cecil, "unfortunately, however, when his servants came to change their evidence, they had been so impressed by their master's desire for green that they had said they saw green at the top, which they could not have done, if it had been a Sharpshooter's uniform."

The result was that the servants were considered by Cochrane's lawyers to be potentially damaging witnesses: if one of them so much as stumbled or hesitated under cross-examination on the colour of the uniform, Cochrane would be instantly discredited in the eyes of the jury.

This is the most likely reason for defence counsel not calling them as witnesses to the colour of the uniform; that, on one hand, they had become unsure just what they did see after their master's prompting of their memories, and on the other, that if their uncertainty showed in the witness box, it would undoubtedly prove fatal. The lawyers, though, now had to find an alternative explanation to present in court and they decided to play the whole matter down and write it off as a "mistake" on Cochrane's part. This at any rate disposed of the difficulty and reduced it solely to a question of whether the jury believed it or not.

So the activities of De Berenger on the morning of the fraud, consistent with the known facts and with regard to the realities of his situation at the time, were most likely as follows: Having successfully spread his false news and returned to Town in the chaise driven by Shilling, he finds himself travelling through the early morning streets of the City soon after daybreak.

In the cold light of day, the audacity he had summoned the previous night to trick unsuspecting and gullible provincials begins to desert him and the seriousness of the crime he has set in train occupies his thoughts during his long, solitary journey. In his portmanteau he carries his green sharpshooter's tunic which he has taken the precaution of bringing as a little insurance policy, for if anything goes wrong, or looks like going wrong with the plan, he would be in a position to attempt an immediate escape out of the country to America on board the *Tonnant* if he could prevail on his easygoing and helpful new acquaintance Lord Cochrane.

Now, increasingly nervous, he begins to feel the need of discarding his false and incriminating persona and to revert to his own identity. Drawing up the blind of the coach, he performs a quick change act, taking off his sword and laying it on the seat of the coach to do so.

At the Marsh Gate, he transfers rapidly into the hackney cab without allowing anyone to get a good look at him and tells Crane to drive him to Grosvenor Square. At this stage he has not defintely decided on visiting Cochrane, since Cochrane Johnstone's house in Great Cumberland Street, and Cochrane's in Green Street are both just a few minutes drive from Grosvenor Square (as indeed is Butt's lodging in Bond Street). As the carriage draws away the bank clerk, Richard Barwick, who knows him slightly, follows behind hoping to hear some news.

Now De Berenger is thoroughly panicked. Did Barwick recognise him at Marsh Gate? Even if he didn't, De Berenger now realises how far out on a limb he is and decides to cash in his insurance policy. He tells Crane to go to Green Street but finds Cochrane is out. He asks to wait and sends out a note requesting him to return but takes the precaution of not signing it, or of signing it only with his initials – the fewer people who know of his arrival the better. The servant returns after a few minutes and says he is unable to find his master.

De Berenger becomes even more edgy and assumes that Cochrane is "not available" in the polite sense, largely because the note was unsigned, so he takes it back, signs it, and asks the servant to try again. When Cochrane returns, De Berenger presses to be allowed to go on board the *Tonnant*. Privately, he feels that he will be safe there, his appointment to drill the sharpshooters perfectly normal and above suspicion.

The ship will also provide him with a free passage to America where he can remain for a year or so. When things have quietened down he can return to England or, failing that, can take up life again in the United States. Cochrane, though, turns him down and tells him he must get permission from Lord Melville and Lord Yarmouth.

De Berenger realises he must resort once more to the streets and to his lodgings but in order not to arouse Cochrane's suspicions about his true reasons for wanting to get out of the country, assures him that he will go immediately to the Admiralty and his superiors.

He tells Cochrane that he cannot appear before Yarmouth and Melville dressed in this way and asks for the loan of a civilian hat.

This does not arouse Cochrane's suspicions because while it would be natural for De Berenger to have his uniform on if he expected to go on board the *Tonnant* immediately in his military capacity, he might be expected to dress as a gentleman rather than an officer to handle a delicate intervew regarding his personal advancement. De Berenger's real motive is that Crane and the servants took notice of him when he got out of the cab and he thinks the green uniform may compromise him.

Cochrane gives him the hat and offers him a coat from the unwanted part of his wardrobe which was being packed for sending on board, whereupon De Berenger changes, wrapping his green tunic "in a towel" since his portmanteau in the hall is otherwise occupied, and disappears back to his lodgings to wait until he has received enough money from Cochrane Johnstone to finance an escape by another route.

By far the most complex part of the evidence was that relating to banknotes. The history of the various cheques Tables and notes was so convoluted that neither prosecuting nor *defence* counsel succeeded in putting it across with complete clarity and Best was evidently confused by it himself.

In essence, the prosecution alleged that there were three cheques involved, the produce of which went to Cochrane, Butt and Cochrane Johnstone, and that some of the notes from each cheque went to De Berenger.

For the purposes of the following explanation, the amounts involved have been rounded off to the nearest pound, but this does not affect the transactions in any material way. Cheque number one was made out for £56 by stock broker Joseph Fearn on 10 February and made payable to Butt. The cheque was changed at the bank for a £50 note, a £5 note 189 and some change. The £50 note was found on De Berenger.

The second cheque was made out by Fearn's clerk on 16 February, made payable to a numbered account and was given to Cochrane. It was for £470. This was changed at the bank for one £200 note, two for £100, a £50 and a £20. Cochrane paid the £50 note to his coal merchant.

The £200 note was changed by Fearn's clerk first into two for £100 and subsequently into 200 £1 notes. Some of these £1 notes were found on De Berenger. The two original £100 were also changed by a clerk of Fearn's into £1 bills and given to Cochrane Johnstone. Some of this lot also turned up in De Berenger's effects.

Cheque number three was made out on 25 February, four days after the fraud, payable to Butt for the sum of £98. This was changed for a £50, a £40, and a £5 plus some coin. The £50 was paid away by De Berenger's servant and the £40 was passed by De Berenger while on the run.

The conclusion drawn by the Stock Exchange was that these transactions represented De Berenger's pay-off from the three main stockholders. It amounted in total, they said, to £540.

Cochrane Johnstone had a plausible explanation of his transactions with De Berenger, but since he was unquestionably guilty, and since it is known that he called on De Berenger with a letter shortly after the fraud and the day before the Prussian disappeared, it may reasonably be inferred that the notes De

Berenger was found with, originating from Cochrane Johnstone were his part of the proceeds as alleged.

The handling of money by Butt cannot be conclusive either way because as the financial agent of the Cochranes and their agent in dealing with Hitchens & Fearn, it was normal for any money in their possession to have gone through his hands first as a matter of course.

The cheques from the brokers were normally made out to Butt who distributed the banknotes for which they were changed to Cochrane and his uncle according to their respective profits.

In addition, Butt also assisted the Cochranes in handling some of their other financial affairs besides stock dealings. If, therefore, any money were put to an improper use by either of the Cochranes, that fact alone could not be evidence against Butt.

Cochrane's explanation of the banknotes was that on 15 February, he borrowed £200 from Butt to complete a stock transaction that had to be closed on the spot. This he repaid four days later with the two £100 notes from the £470 which was the profit on that same transaction.

Soon after, he visited a wine merchant where he ordered a large stock of wines for the *Tonnant*. On the 22 or 23 February he asked Butt to settle the wine account and certain other outstanding bills for him and gave him £1,200 which included the £200 note from the £470 cheque. The next day, Butt handed over to Cochrane Johnstone some money from the stock account, using the banknotes he had on hand, and this included the notes which Cochrane had given him earlier.

By this means, the large notes from the £470 draft ended up in Cochrane Johnstone's hands, and went from there to De Berenger. Cochrane pointed out that at no stage were the £1 notes,found on De Berenger, in his possession as shown at the trial. He also pointed out that, according to the prosecutors, of the £540 pay-off allegedly made to De Berenger, £400 came from himself.

Since he made only £1,700 while Butt and Cochrane Johnstone together made £4,800, this would seem to be a rather inequitable arrangement.

One of the most telling points that Cochrane's counsel had at his disposal during the trial was that the Stock Exchange only got De Berenger's name in the first place from Cochrane's affidavit. If true, this claim would go a long way to support his innocence. The Stock Exchange subcommittee evidently thought so too, for in January 1815, some six months after the trial, they published another report on the whole affair, tying up loose ends and publicising their successful prosecution.

In this report, they said that not only were they aware that Du Bourg and De Berenger were the same five days before Cochrane mentioned the name, but that a warrant was already out against De Berenger, and moreover that one of the witnesses was eventually paid the reward. In saying this, some or all of the men who composed the subcommittee showed that they considered the matter of sufficient importance to publish an incorrect version of the facts. The correct version is, as described earlier, that William Harrison gave De Berenger's name to the subcommittee on 8 March, three days before Cochrane's affidavit, but the information was not acted upon until the day Cochrane swore the affidavit. This may have been because previous witnesses had also given names to the subcommittee: on 4 March Michael Gorman offered James Bourke, who it seemed habitually used the alias "Du Bourg", and earlier still Thomas Vinn had given them Alexander McRae who fitted the description of the Dover impostor.

The claim that they had already taken out a warrant for De Berenger's arrest is also incorrect. The warrant was issued by the Alien Department of the Home Office, under whose licence De Berenger was resident in England, not *before* the publication of the affidavit, but five days after, on 17 March. Indeed, the grounds for his arrest were that although his licence permitted him to live in England, it did not permit him to leave the country, and this suggests that while they had his name, they did not yet have any evidence against him.

The statement that a witness was eventually given the reward cannot be substantiated by reference to the records of the subcommittee. From these it appears that a total of £101 was paid to Thomas Vinn for putting the finger on McRae, that 100 guineas was voted to buy a piece of plate for presentation to Germain Lavie for his handling of the case, and a further 20 guineas in tips for the solictor's clerks.

No other sums are mentioned in the minutes despite the fact that they carry on until after the date of publication of the report now in question. That other payments were made and went unrecorded is highly probable but it seems that Vinn's was the largest reward and certainly no-one is mentioned as claiming the 250 guineas advertised for Du Bourg's arrest and conviction.

With regard to Cochrane's guilt or innocence, there are really three questions to be considered: did he receive a fair deal? Was the evidence sufficient for the conviction actually obtained? And finally, was he actually guilty?

On the first count, it can be said with certainty that he did not receive a fair deal. He got no help whatever from the Admiralty and though this was entirely through his own fault it contributed materially to his downfall.

Far from helping him, the Admiralty recommended his enemy Germain Lavie to the Stock Exchange. It is also true that the barrister he consulted about taking legal action against the Stock Exchange, John Gurney, later appeared for the prosecution at the trial and knew at least in part what Cochrane's defence would be. His own counsel did depart from his instructions, over the colour of the uniform and the giving of a disguise. Evidence was manipulated by the prosecution, for example the Dover letter and the date of buying stocks, to put the defendants in the worst light. Above all the judge showed strong bias for the prosecution and against the defendants time and again. Among the worst manifestations of his partialitywere forcing the defence to open at 10 at night after a 13-hour sitting, and the misquoting evidence to the jury in his summing up.

On the second count also, it is possible to say quite definitely that Cochrane should not have been convicted on the evidence presented. It simply was not enough and left too many questions unanswered – such as the question of his motive. What convicted him was not the body of evidence brought against him but the climate of opinion produced by the prosecuting counsel and, more importantly, by the judge. When Lord Ellenborough told the jury that "If he (De Berenger) appeared in such an habit, he must have appeared to any rational person fully blazoned in the costume of that or some other crime", together with his observation that De Berenger had no means of changing tunics, he was in effect telling them to convict Cochrane.

The third question, was Cochrane really guilty? cannot ever be answered with absolute and complete certainty, because there is always the chance, however slim, that the greatest and most honourable man in the world may one day feel an irrational and ungovernable urge to slip one of his host's silver spoons into his pocket – and Cochrane was far from being a saint.

But the question can be answered beyond a reasonable doubt by dispassionate reference to the evidence and without the distracting promptings of a Lord Ellenborough.

Those who believe Cochrane was guilty must accept as a logical consequence the proposition that a senior naval officer and Member of Parliament, of high character and reputation, without any motive, committed the grave crime of sending a false dispatch to the Admiralty in time of war, jeopardising his career in the navy and public life and the great financial prospects and challenge of an important new command. And that he subsequently told the whole world of his crime and his accomplice in an affidavit.

This is a proposition I cannot accept. It is quite simply beyond the bounds of probability. Cochrane had nothing to gain by being party to the fraud and everything to lose. Given the circumstance that the swindle of the previous year had provoked cries for blood from the City, and that the Stock Exchange could be expected to come down hard on any new attempt to defraud investors, the fraud of 1814 was the act of desperate men: men like De Berenger and Cochrane Johnstone.

It was not the act of a rich young nobleman and Member of Parliament, at the peak of his career, with a new young wife, a son on the way, and an important service to perform. On the evidence available, Lord Cochrane, I believe, was innocent of complicity in the fraud on the Stock Exchange.

CHAPTER EIGHT
Flag of Convenience

"A skilful rifleman ought to be steady, cool, patient, self-possessed, active, bold, and observant both of effects and causes."

Charles Random De Berenger "Helps and Hints How to Protect Life, Property &tc."

The events of February and June 1814 were quickly swept aside by the tide of rejoicing following Napoleon's defeat and exile, and the ending of war after more than two decades.

Inconstant public fancy exchanged without a second thought the plight of its naval hero for the glittering spectacle of the Czar's state visit to London augmented by lavish victory celebrations following years of public austerity. Cochrane, De Berenger and the rest were yesterday's news and were quickly forgotten.

The indestructible Prussian disappeared from the glare of publicity for some years, but jauntily re-emerged in the 1830's, having elevated himself to the rank of Lieutenant Colonel, and launching his most grandiose scheme, the opening of Cremorne public gardens in Chelsea and its main attraction, The Stadium. Here, according to the prospectus, London's nobility and gentry were able to enjoy "The retirements of rural life; at the very elbow of the now most fashionable parts of the metropolis; the greater portion of these picturesque promenades being adorned by the plantation of superior evergreen, and decorative and agreeable constructions, contrasted by magnificent timber, diffusing luxurious shade over extensive pleasure grounds."

At the sporting Stadium they were able to "cultivate various skilful and manly exercises" including shooting, gymnastics and swimming in the nearby Thames. These lofty pursuits rapidly gave way to activities of a more commercial if no less invigorating nature and after changing hands several times, Cremorne was closed down by outraged officialdom in the 1870's for "irregularities" – the Victorian euphemism for whoring on the grand scale.

Cremorne's luxuriantly shaded and extensive pleasure grounds are today commemorated by the Lott's Road power station.

The enterprising Baron enshrined his philosophy (or perhaps his assessment of the critical faculties of his paying customers) in the motto of his grand undertaking: *Volenti nihil difficile* (roughly speaking, Nothing is impossible for he who has the will). He also bent his will to a sideline as an author and penned the work from which the chapter headings of this book are taken, "*Helps and Hints How to Protect Life, Property &tc.*" This distillation of his experience of the dangers besetting the gentleman at large, written to a (presumably) fictional nephew, Augustus, is in many ways an unconscious expression of the pitfalls of his own career.

His regiment, the Duke of Cumberland's Sharpshooters, was disbanded in 1814 but continued to exist as a private rifle club, the Royal Victoria Rifle Company, which was eventually accepted for service as the 1st Middlesex Rifle Volunteers in 1859. In 1908, the unit became part of Queen Victoria's Rifles, and until as recently as 2007 was represented by the Headquarters Company, 4th Volunteer Battalion, the Royal Green Jackets.

After selling off Cremorne, and making a little money for his old age, he retired at last to take his ease and sire a large family.

Andrew Cochrane Johnstone, too, withdrew from the vicissitudes of London life, though with rather less dignity and rather more haste. He disappeared permanently, almost certainly back to the happy hunting grounds of the West Indies, where he was pursued tenaciously but without success, by an irate Richard Butt.

The money that they made on the venerable 21 February 1814, amounting to well over £8,000, was eventually distributed by the Stock Exchange Committee to a long list of deserving charities. The Committee also unanimously voted a sum of money to buy a piece of plate for presentation to its solicitor, Germain Lavie, as an expression of gratitude for his handling of the case, as well as lesser sums as gratuities for his clerks.

In the end, only the poor and members of the legal profession were enriched by the biggest fraud in history.

Cochrane, his career in ruins, threw himself with even greater ferocity into attacking public corruption, and he joined with Sir Francis Burdett in the House to make life uncomfortable for the establishment. For a man of such energy and action, though, the steady grind of the Commons was a poor substitute for the lightning decision and turbulent activity of the quarterdeck and he ached for command at sea again.

In 1818 his prayer was answered in the unlikely form of the Chilean ambassador, Don Jose Alvarez, who came to London to raise cash and support for his fledgling country's attempt to throw off Spanish Imperial rule.

On land, Chile's patriot army had already shown itself a match for the military might of its former masters but what the country lacked was any effective form of sea power. In Cochrane, Alvarez thought he had found the answer to his problem. His offer to Cochrane was irresistible: no less than command of the embryo Chilean Navy.

Cochrane's answer was immediate and in the affirmative. Other officers, too, were attracted to South America in the slump following the end of war with France and the Government pushed through a foreign enlistment act in an attempt to stop Cochrane and others like him from signing up with overseas states. For Cochrane, though, already dismissed from the service in his own country, the act was meaningless and he sailed in November 1818 for the Pacific.

Shortly after his arrival he was appointed Vice-Admiral of Chile, Admiral and Commander-in-Chief of the Naval Forces of the Republic, under the Captain-General and Supremo of Chile, Bernado O'Higgins. The Navy over which he presided was a motley affair of some half dozen ships with which he set out confident as ever to destroy the Spanish fleet.

The strongest position held by the Spanish was the heavily fortified and garrisoned province of Valdivia. Cochrane assaulted and captured the town early in 1820 and effectively broke the Spanish grip on Chile at a single stroke.

The following year he accepted an invitation from Brazil to help them fight the Portuguese and after creating from scratch the Brazilian Navy he cleared their seas of Portuguese ships with his accustomed style, taking over 100 enemy vessels and vast quantities of stores, ammunition and gold with a single ship and without losing a man.

After returning from South America, and a brief flirtation with the Greek Navy in the cause of that country's independence, Cochrane took his family and lived in Paris for a few years.

By 1831 he was over 55 and his days of daring exploits were over, but at last the tide of luck turned in his personal life. William IV was now on the throne, Wellington's Tory administration was replaced by Grey's Whig Government and Henry Brougham, his friend and advocate of 1814, became Lord Chancellor.

His father died that same year and he succeeded to the title as 10th Earl of Dundonald. With the combination of a monarch who was a sailor, and a Lord Chancellor who was a friend and political ally, Cochrane now stood a realistic chance of becoming rehabilitated. In 1828 he had addressed a memorandum to the Duke of Clarence, then Lord High Admiral and later to ascend the throne – asking to be re-instated, but received the answer that the King's Cabinet could not comply with his prayer. In 1830, he tried once more but again without success.

Some time later, Lady Cochrane gained an audience with King William to plead her husband's cause. Presumably she was successful in this because in March 1832 he was at last granted a free pardon, and two months later was re-instated in the Navy with the rank of Rear-Admiral. It was still a source of complaint with him, though, that he was not restored to the Order of the Bath or offered financial compensation and he pressed the King and Admiralty for full restitution.

When Victoria succeeded to the throne in 1837 his continued pressure began to yield results and in 1841 he was awarded a Government pension for meritorious service and promoted to Vice-Admiral. In 1847 he was eventually re-instated in the Order of the Bath and finally, at the age of 72 was given command at sea once more when he was appointed to the West Indies Station as commander-in-chief.

He occupied his remaining years with plans for secret weapons and with his memoirs. He died in 1860 at the age of 85 and was buried in Westminster Abbey.

At the request of Queen Victoria, his banner was restored to King Henry VII Chapel the day before his funeral, the final act of restitution.

The question might legitimately be asked, does it matter now whether Cochrane was innocent or guilty of complicity in the Stock Exchange fraud? I believe it does matter for two reasons.

First, the worst kind of injustice is one which goes unrecorded and is thus allowed to pass quietly into history with no blame attaching to its authors. Although Cochrane was pardoned and restored to rank, he was never formally acquitted and the consequences of his conviction both for himself and his country were irreparably damaging.

Second, and more important, is Cochrane's place in a historical context. In the early years of the Nineteenth Century, the position of England with regard to Napoleon's France was very much like her position in 1940 with regard to Hitler's Germany. The Emperor ruled over the Continent, his army was the most powerful in the world and the invasion barges were loading at Calais. In 1940, Britain was saved by the Few – a handful of courageous young men whose almost superhuman efforts kept the Luftwaffe from the skies. So in the early 1800's it was the Few who kept Bonaparte from Britain's shores.

In the words of Pitt, "only Nelson and the fleet stand between us and Bonaparte".

Cochrane was one of those earlier Few; young naval captains whose courage and seamanship alone prevented the French from dominating England as they had much of the rest of Europe. It would be unworthy of his efforts and sacrifices if the liberator of Chile and Brazil were not also remembered as one of the most tireless and indomitable defenders of his own country.

NOTES

1. The telegraph at this time was a semaphore device which required good visibility to be operated. In clear conditions it was capable of relaying a message from Deal to the Admiralty in London in less than half an hour.

2. Not entirely though: the Accountant General to the Court of Chancery took the plunge in Consols to the tune of nearly £16,000.

3. In total, the three men sold Omnium and Consols amounting to £1.6 millions.

4. In the lengthy article he wrote attempting to clear his name published in *Cobbett's Political Register* for 26 March 1814, p 408.

5. The banknote evidence was the most complex part of the case and here Best was either confusing himself or confusing the jury because he dealt only with one lot of £200. This question is examined in more detail in Chapter Seven.

6. Lord Melville. First Lord of the Admiralty.

7. Peace talks between the allies and French.

8. It was a blazing June day.

9. A Matter of Speculation

10. This comment by the judge is now seen to be doubly unwarranted in the light of the fact that the letter was not written at the Ship Inn.

11. Ellenborough, The Guilt of Lord Cochrane in 1814.

12. A Matter Of Speculation.

BIBLIOGRAPHY

The Trial of Charles Random De Berenger, Lord Cochrane and Others for conspiracy to defraud the Stock Exchange. Transcript by W.B.Gurney, London, 1814.

Minutes of Stock Exchange subcommittee formed to investigate the frauds of 1813 and 1814. Manuscript, Stock Exchange archives.

Report of Stock Exchange subcommittee, March 1814. Stock Exchange archives.

The Case Against All Defendants. Manuscript instructions to prosecuting counsel, Stock Exchange archives, 1814.

Secret Memoirs of the Honourable Andrew Cochrane Johnstone etc. Pamphlet. A Mackenrot, London 1814.

Cobbett's Political Register, March 26 1814.

A Letter to Lord Ellenborough from Lord Cochrane. London, 1815 . Pamphlet.

Report of the Stock Exchange subcommittee, January 1815. London, 1815.

The Noble Stockjobber. 1816. Charles Random De Berenger, London

Trial of Lord Cochrane for escaping from prison. Hone. London, 1816.

Trials of R.G. Butt for Libel. R.G. Butt, London 1817.

Helps and Hints How to Protect Life, Property &tc., Charles Random De Berenger, London, 1835.

Observations on Naval Affairs. Pamphlet. London 1847. Thomas, Lord Dundonald.

Autobiography of a Seaman, London, 1860, Thomas, Lord Dundonald.

Law Magazine and Review, February 1861. Review of Autobiography of a Seaman and reply. Re-printed and published, London, 1817.

Memorials, Personal and Historical of Admiral Lord Gambier, Lady Chatterton, London, 1861.

Life of Dundonald. Anonymous (attributed to MacGilchrist). London, 1861.

The Trial of Lord Cochrane Before Lord Ellenborough. J.B.Atlay. Smith, Elder & Co., London 1897.

The Guilt of Lord Cochrane in 1814, Lord Ellenborough. Smith, Elder & Co. London, 1914.

Sir Francis Burdett and His Times 1770-1844. M.W.Patterson, Macmillan, London, 1931.

The Naval Heritage, David Mathews, Collins, London, 1944.

Lord Cochrane, Christopher Lloyd, Longmans, London, 1947.

Extraordinary Seaman, J.P.W.Mallalieu, MacGibbon & Kee, London, 1957,

Cochrane: A Life of Admiral The Earl of Dundonald. Warren Tute, Cassell, London, 1965.

A Matter of Speculation, Henry Cecil, Hutchinson, London, 1965.

The Navy in Transition, Michael Lewis, Hodder and Stoughton, London, 1965.

Books by Richard Milton

The Ministry of Spin

When the Second World War ended in 1945, the Government's propaganda offensive was only just beginning. But now its target was the British people. The Ministry of Spin tells the story of how the post-war Labour government contrived to retain, in secret, much of the wartime Ministry Of Information, how they buried this powerful propaganda machine deep in Whitehall. And how they turned these wartime propaganda powers on the British Parliament, media and people to push through their political programme.

Shattering the Myths of Darwinism

The controversial best-seller that provides compelling evidence that the most important assumptions on which Darwinism rests are scientifically wrong. Milton exposes the gaping holes in an ideology that has reigned unchallenged over the scientific world for a century and shows that the theory of evolution has become an act of faith rather than a functioning science. He argues for a fresh scientific approach to evolutionary biology that does not depend on blind chance.

Best of Enemies

A stunning popular history of 100 years (1845-1945) of Anglo-German love/hate, exposing the secrets of a relationship steeped in mutual admiration, blood and propaganda. During two world wars, Germany, Britain and the USA spent billions on clandestine propaganda to blacken each other's reputations, giving birth to the PR industry itself. Richard Milton's expertly written popular history gives a fresh perspective on this tumultuous, painful love-hate relationship, and is also a brilliant study of propaganda itself.

Forbidden Science

This compelling tour through the world of anomalous research, makes clear what the scientific establishment takes pains to deny: plenty of hard experimental evidence already exists for such things as cold fusion, paranormal phenomena, bioenergy and the effectiveness of alternative medicine. Because these subjects and those who dare to investigate them are continually denied legitimacy by what can only be called the "paradigm police," the public is led to believe that all claims made about such topics are completely groundless. With humour and an eye for the telling detail, the author describes many instances when the defenders of scientific orthodoxy acted with unscientific rigidity in the face of the evidence. Milton discusses the forces at work in the marginalisation of unorthodox research and makes us wonder if there isn't something deeply wrong with the way that science is currently practiced.

Bad Company

Bad Company explains why some of the world's largest companies sometimes behave in insanely self-defeating ways, jeopardising their reputations and public image. The most famous corporations in the world recline at their peril on the analyst's couch in this unique investigation into the corporate unconscious mind. Providing insights into corporate behaviour and their relationships with the public, based on the premise that companies operate from motives of which they are scarcely consciously aware.

Fiction

Dead Secret. Investigative journalist Tony Gabriel stumbles onto his biggest ever story when he inherits the papers of a long-dead historian – and finds himself the target of an ancient secret society. Are they just rich, powerful people playing an elaborate game, or have they truly gained paranormal powers to see into the future?

"Following the convolutions of this novel requires as close a focus as chasing a coiling anaconda along the jungle floor, but is far more exciting and entertaining." **Mallory Heart**

"Different isn't always good. In this instance, it was. Dead Secret is a unique and clever story that provided an entertaining and at times thought-provoking read." **BigAl, Books and Pals**

"Dead Secret will ensnare your senses and lead you down a path from which there may be no release." **Star**

The Glass Harmonica Concert pianist Julia Franklin is heir to an inheritance worth a billion dollars – enough to bankrupt America's oldest bank when the trust matures. Miles Bartholemew, of Bartholemew's Bank. has to find the heirs of the Franklin trust and deal with them permanently, before his family's bank is ruined.

"It's not often I give 5 stars to any book. I simply ignored everything I had to do and sat and read it all the way through." **Books R Best**

Conjuring For Beginners When legendary con-artist Ferdy Daniels dies alone and penniless, his daughter, Rosa, inherits his victims, who are convinced she was his partner in crime. To keep one jump ahead of them – and stay alive – Rosa must unravel Ferdy's web of deceits. But to re-trace her father's footsteps, she must learn to become as quick-witted and cunning as Ferdy, the master magician.

"I had already read Dead Secret by the same author and liked it, but I liked this even more." **Nicoletta**

True Stories: Mysteries of Crime and Punishment. Every story in this book is true – except one. Some tell of crimes that have gone unpunished by the law. Some are crimes against laws that are unwritten. And some are crimes that exist only in the mind.

"Where Richard takes us with these true stories is into the interstices of the criminal mind and the events that build toward dastardly events. He weaves these stories with a blend of sex and human weakness and blunders that approach humour - both sides of the drama mask. They make very fine reading - recommended."
Grady Harp

Printed in Great Britain
by Amazon

21035989R00093